The 500 Hidden Secrets of

MADRID

D0808126

INTRODUCTION

As one would expect from a European capital with such a rich history, Madrid has a lot of culture, beautiful architecture and wonderful restaurants to wow its visitors. This guide of course includes those selling points, like 5 stunning palaces, 5 buildings from the time of *los Austrias,* and 5 fusion restaurants that are worth a visit. But while respecting its traditions – for example the 5 churches and cathedrals to admire – the city also has managed to embrace modern times, with cool coffee bars and trendy shops; it is in fact one of the best shopping destinations in Europe. With this guide in your backpack, you're all set to discover this hipper side of the city as well, for example 5 buzzing after work bars or the flagship stores of 5 innovative Spanish brands.

Like the rest of the country, Madrid went through some rocky years after the economic crisis hit in 2008, but has recovered gracefully. The city council succeeded in bringing the necessary change, in order to position Madrid not only as the country's political capital and business destination, but also, and especially, as a cultural hub. The city is very dedicated to enhance the quality of life of its inhabitants, with the greatest respect for the environment, by making green and sustainable choices.

In any case, the people of Madrid never lost their happy spirit and their love of socialising over a beer, not even during the worst moments of the economic crisis. In fact it's the optimism of its habitants that makes Madrid move forward so fast. This guide was written to help visitors experience this positive vibe, which comes to life in the different neighbourhoods. From Centro to Retiro, from Salamanca to Chamberí: each of these districts has a distinctive look-and-feel, a unique character formed by the secrets that this book aims to reveal.

HOW TO USE THIS BOOK?

This guide lists 500 things you need to know about Madrid in 100 different categories. Most of these are places to visit, with practical information like the address and sometimes info on making reservations. Others are bits of information that help you get to know the city and its people. The purpose of this guide is to inspire you to explore the city, but it doesn't cover every aspect from A to Z.

The places in this guide are given an address, including the neighbourhood (for example 'Chamberí' or 'Retiro'), and a number. The neighbourhood and number allow you to find the places on the maps at the beginning of the book: first look for the map of the corresponding neighbourhood, then look for the right number. A word of caution however: these maps are not detailed enough to allow you to find specific locations in the city. They are included to give you a sense of where places are, and whether they are close by other places of interest. You can obtain an excellent map from any tourist office or in most hotels. Or the addresses can be located on a smartphone.

Please also bear in mind that cities change all the time. The chef who hits a high note one day may be uninspiring on the day you happen to visit. The hotel ecstatically reviewed in this book might suddenly go downhill under a new manager. The bar considered one of the 5 amazing rooftop bars might be empty on the night you're there. This is obviously a highly personal selection. You might not always agree with it. If you want to leave a comment, recommend a bar or reveal your favourite secret place, please visit the website *www.the500hiddensecrets.com* – you'll also find free tips and the latest news about the series there – or follow *@500hiddensecrets* on Instagram and leave a comment.

THE AUTHOR

Anna-Carin Nordin is a true world citizen: she's Swedish, but she was born and raised in Lausanne (Switzerland) and later moved to Barcelona where she lived for 5 years. In 2001 she decided to settle in Madrid. Today she lives there together with her husband (a true Madrilène), while also spending time in their second home in Miami, Florida.

Anna-Carin made a career in the hospitality industry; she is the founder of The Hotel Anthropologist *(www.hotelanthropologist.com)* and she teaches Entrepreneurship in the Master in Hospitality & Tourism program at EADA (Barcelona). She is also the co-founder of *www.notable-notebooks.com,* a result of her love for aesthetics and design.

Writing this guide made Anna-Carin fall in love with Madrid all over again, feeling more happy and sure than ever about her decision to settle there. She especially loves the city's elegance and diversity, from the impressive architecture of the 19th century to the bohemian atmosphere of neighbourhoods such as Malasaña. Curious and passionate, she finds herself at home in a city that is so vibrant and open-minded. Madrid has indeed so much to offer for someone who, like her, is always on the lookout for the latest trends and new restaurants and cuisines she can try out.

Anna-Carin Nordin wants to especially thank her husband Jordi, who always supports and encourages her with all her new endeavours. They say that home is where the heart is; Anna-Carin's heart is definitely in Madrid.

MADRID

overview

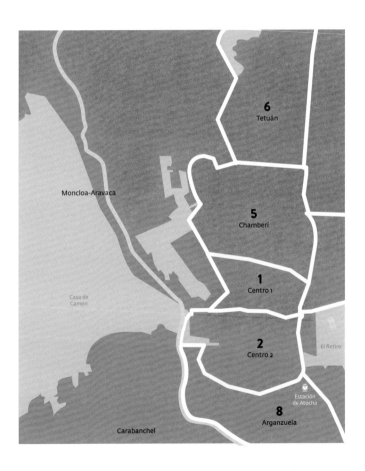

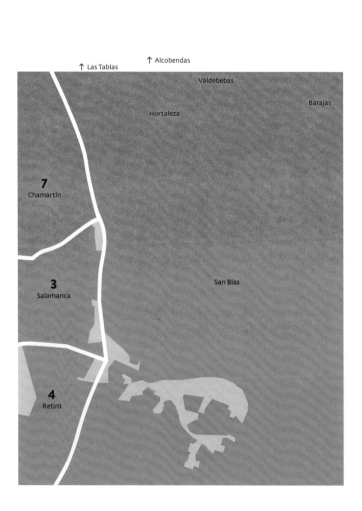

↑ Las Tablas

↑ Alcobendas

Valdebebas

Barajas

Hortaleza

7
Chamartín

3
Salamanca

San Blas

4
Retiro

Map 1
CENTRO 1

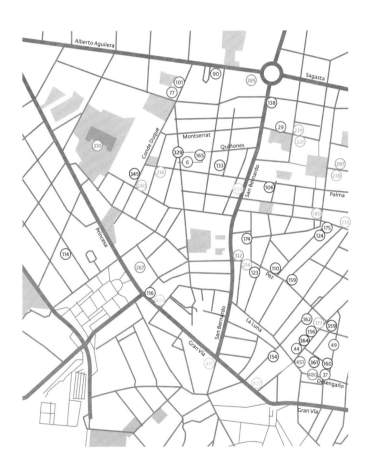

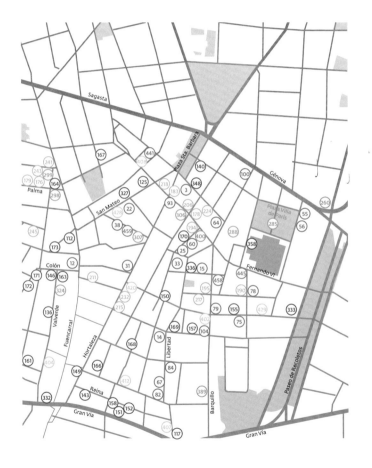

Map 2
CENTRO 2

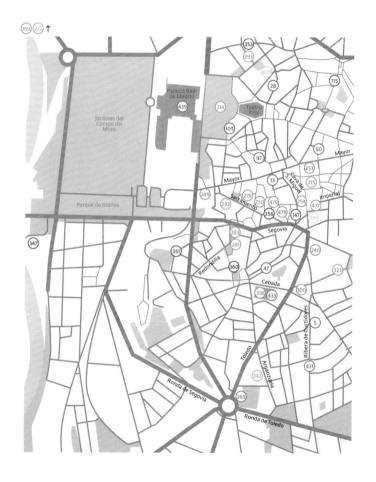

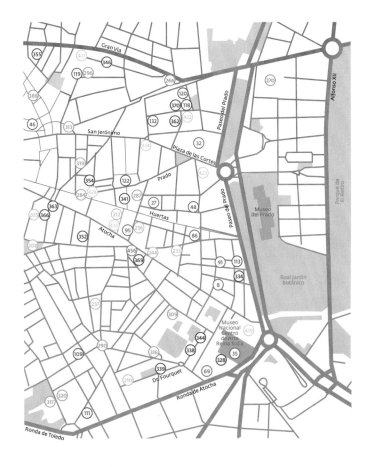

Map 3

SALAMANCA

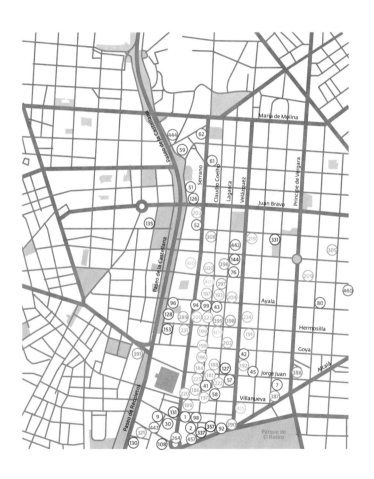

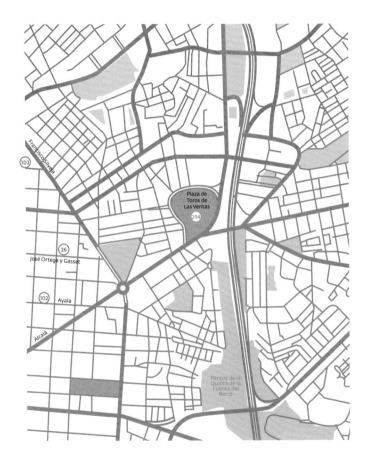

Map 4
RETIRO

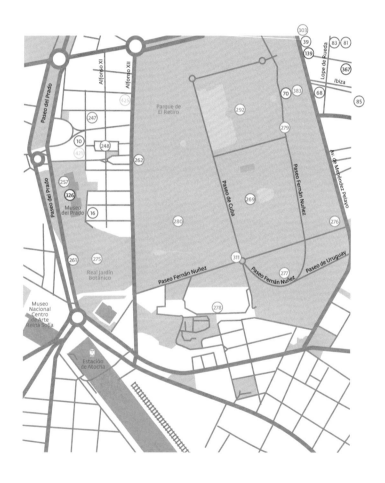

Map 5
CHAMBERÍ

Map 6
TETUÁN

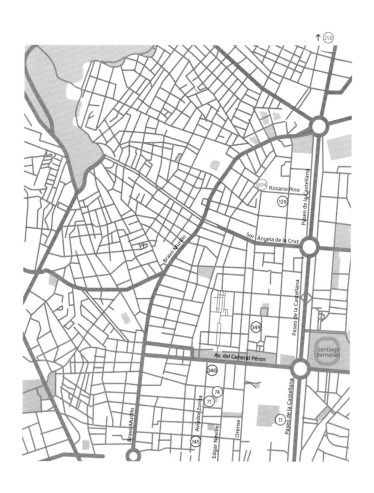

Map 7
CHAMARTÍN

Map 8
ARGANZUELA

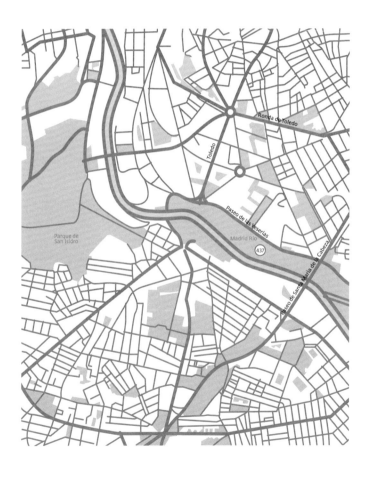

LA CARMENCITA

105 PLACES TO EAT OR BUY GOOD FOOD

The 5 nicest places to have **BREAKFAST** —————— 24

The 5 best **BRUNCHES** *to enjoy on weekends*—————— 26

The 5 best **MARKETS** *to grab a bite* —————— 28

5 great places to have **LUNCH** —————— 30

5 places for **HEALTHY FOOD**
to eat in or take out—————— 32

Top 5 **VEGGIE** *restaurants* —————— 34

The 5 nicest **TERRACES** *to dine alfresco* —————— 36

The 5 best places for **SANDWICHES** —————— 38

5 places to enjoy **IBERIC HAM** —————— 40

5 **MADRID CLASSICS** *loved by the locals* —————— 42

5 restaurants to **EAT AND PARTY**
UNTIL 3 AM —————— 45

The 5 latest **HOTSPOTS** ———————— 47

5 **TRENDY** *and* **AFFORDABLE** *places* ———— 49

5 **INNOVATIVE** *restaurant concepts*———— 51

5 great restaurants for **GALICIAN**
and **BASQUE** *specialities* ———————— 53

5 restaurants for **CENTRAL** *and*
LATIN AMERICAN FOOD ————————— 55

The 5 best **TABERNAS** *for tapas and more* ———— 57

5 **FUSION RESTAURANTS** *worth a visit* ——— 59

5 places for your **AFTERNOON**
SUGAR KICK ————————————— 61

5 of the best **DELIS** *in town* ——————— 63

The 5 best **BAKERIES** ————————— 65

The 5 nicest places to have
BREAKFAST

---

1 MALLORCA

Serrano 6
Salamanca ③
+34 915 771 859
www.pasteleria-
mallorca.com

Madrid's first pastry shop. Opened in 1931 and ever since then they have been serving the best *ensaimadas* (a typical sweet bread from the Island of Mallorca) in town. The Serrano Café has the best location with a nice terrace to observe the crowd coming from Salamanca while sipping your coffee and enjoying an assortment of finger sandwiches.

2 MAGASAND

Columela 4
Salamanca ③
+34 915 768 843
www.magasand.com

At Magasand everything is healthy. The menu features everything from sandwiches to acai bowls and fresh fruit juices. Because of the restaurant's minimalist industrial interiors, it tends to attract creative minds on their morning break.

3 CRIPEKA

Santa Teresa 2
Centro ①
+34 911 99 91 08

This place started out as a take-out joint but thanks to the charming and colourful interior you feel compelled to sit down and start the day with one of their signature sandwiches and their homemade cakes. And if the setting doesn't quite do it for you, then know that everything is always available to take out.

4   CRUSTÓ

Gaztambide 3
Chamberí ⑤
+34 910 513 299
www.crusto.es

The smell of fresh bread will hypnotise you as you enter Crustó. With 14 different types of bread, pastries and sandwiches, there are plenty of breakfast options to choose from. The interior is sophisticated with a retro feel to it. A great place to gently kick-start your day.

5   MARTINA COCINA

Plaza de Cascorro 11
Centro ②
+34 910 834 380
www.martinacocina.es

Martina, who originally hails from Argentina, will personally take care of your breakfast. She bakes cakes, quiches and her famous *dulce de leche* cookies in the open kitchen. The light, unfussy interior attracts a young and hip local crowd. On sunny days, all the windows on the street side are thrown open, so a nice breeze wakes you up as you sip your coffee.

4 CRUSTÓ

The 5 best
B R U N C H E S
to enjoy on weekends

---

6   FEDERAL CAFÉ

**Plaza de las
Comendadoras 9**
Centro ①
+34 915 328 424
www.federalcafe.es

They serve organic food for small or hearty appetites on brunch day. Their avocado toast comes highly recommended along with their signature morning burger. The restaurant is drenched in natural light, has a functional Nordic interior, good service and amazing homemade cakes.

7   FONTI

Castelló 12
Salamanca ③
+34 917 526 583
www.fontymadrid.com

At Fonti the croissant is simply perfect and the pastries are too good to resist. The setting is inspired by coffee places on the East Coast mixing wood with turquoise and white. Finally, their brunch menu with either Eggs Benedict or a burger makes your choice even easier on languorous weekend mornings.

8   GANZ CAFÉ

Almadén 9
Centro ②
+34 911 733 937
www.ganzcafe.com

Nestled in Las Letras, Ganz is a tiny oasis of bohemian charm and good taste. They pay attention to detail and that's obvious from what they serve. The brunch is for early birds as it is served until 2 pm but it comes with a nice selection of main courses, combined with fruit juices and sweet treats.

9 **LA JEFA**

Recoletos 14
Salamanca ③
+34 916 217 674
www.lajefamadrid.
com

With cosy and welcoming interiors, La Jefa has a very colonial ambiance. Brunch is served from 11 am until 1 pm and includes a wide array of traditional and exotic dishes. Eggs Benedict, Mediterranean mezzes or *cachapa* (pancakes) of corn are just a few of the menu items. Your two dishes come with fresh bread, marmalade and a good coffee to kickstart your day.

10 **RITZ**

Plaza de la Lealtad 5
Retiro ④
+34 917 016 883
www.mandarin
oriental.es/ritzmadrid

A real five-star brunch! Decadently luxurious and traditional at the same time, the Ritz is probably the most unique place you'll ever have brunch at. The buffet includes paella, roast beef and sushi and will definitely keep you busy for a few hours. Eat to the accompaniment of live music. You can also sit on the terrace or in the garden.

8 GANZ CAFÉ

The 5 best
MARKETS
to grab a bite

———————

11 **MADREAT**
Paseo de la
Castellana 89
Tetuán ⑥
www.madreat.org

Every third weekend of the month, the best food trucks gather here. Throw in some good music and a relaxed ambiance and you get one of the best food gatherings in Madrid. Take advantage of the opportunity to taste some of the signature dishes of famous Madrid restaurants such as Chifa, Arzabal, Triciclo and Kabuki.

12 **SAN ILDEFONSO**
Fuencarral 57
Centro ①
+34 915 591 300
www.mercado
desanildefonso.com

Any time during the day and night is a good opportunity to grab a bite with a beer at San Ildefonso market. Here you will find a wide range of traditional Spanish street food including *croquetas*, Spanish omelette and seafood. And yes, burgers too of course! The market's industrial interior is similar to that of Chelsea Market in New York.

13 SAN MIGUEL

Plaza de San
Miguel s/n
Centro ②
+34 915 424 936
*www.mercado
desanmiguel.es*

Not only is it one of the oldest in town but it is also considered the precursor of the culinary market in Madrid. The original structure was built in 1916 and refurbished in 2009 and is one of the most popular places for a round of Tapas and a glass of wine. Take some time to walk around and discover every stall before taking your pick.

14 SAN ANTÓN

Augusto Figueroa 24
Centro ①
+34 913 300 730
*www.mercado
sananton.com*

San Antón has a market where you can buy all kinds of delicacies on the ground floor, a food court on the second floor and a rooftop terrace on the third floor. In summer, the rooftop is a perfect place for an aperitivo with a view over the roofs of Madrid.

15 EL HUERTO DE LUCAS

San Lucas 13
Centro ①
+34 915 135 466
*www.elhuerto
delucas.com*

Sustainability is the key word at Huerto de Lucas and it all started when they converted an old garage into an eco-marketplace and restaurant. 450 square meters of food options, based on 3 principles: everything must be organic, fresh and of high quality.

5 great places to have
LUNCH

16 **MURILLO CAFÉ**
Ruiz de Alarcón 27
Retiro ④
+34 913 693 689
www.murillocafe.com

A bohemian bistro with a Mediterranean inspired menu that literally caters to any palate: from salads to tapas and burgers, you name it, they have it. Try their home-made carrot cake! On sunny days, sit in their small outdoor area, which overlooks the Prado Museum. A busy local brunch spot on weekends.

17 **CASA CIRO**
Fernando el Santo 4
Chamberí ⑤
+34 911 386 233
www.casaciro.es

A modern tavern inspired by the past. The setting is relaxed and offers formal seating or a stool at the bar. The tiles make the interior so fetching, combining green with vegetable motifs and black and white for the floor. The food is straightforward and respectful of tradition.

18 **EL INVERNADERO DE LOS PEÑOTES**
Carretera de Burgos, km 13 Alcobendas
+34 911 385 725
www.elinvernaderode lospenotes.es

The 15-minute taxi ride from the centre is well worth the hassle. Set in the Los Peñotes garden centre, El Invernadero (the greenhouse) is one the most extraordinary interior design projects you'll ever see. The space is colourful, modern, romantic and surprising. The traditional Spanish bistro food is just as amazing as the setting.

19 **FISMULER**
Sagasta 29
Chamberí ⑤
+34 918 277 581
www.fismuler.es

After all the unnecessary elements have been stripped away, all that remains is good food and a nice ambiance. Here, the emphasis is on the food, which for the most part consists of fish and vegetables. Fismuler subtly mixes Nordic culinary influences with Spanish products, as evidenced in their signature dish called 'Sea and Mountain'.

20 **LA VAQUERIA MONTANESA**
Blanca de Navarra 8
Chamberí ⑤
+34 911 387 106
www.lavaqueria montanesa.es

Located in a former 19th-century dairy, which sold products from Cantabria, this restaurant has become an embassy for traditional high quality products. The simple and minimalist interior inspires you to look at what's on your plate instead. Enjoy some Ottolenghi-inspired antipasti or northern recipes during your lunch break.

20 LA VAQUERIA MONTANESA

5 places for
HEALTHY FOOD
to eat in or take out

---

21 FIT FOOD
Génova 25
Chamberí ⑤
+34 917 372 989
www.fitfood.es

This is the temple of cold pressed eco fruit juices and detox cures. Here you can buy a one-week juice detox programme or enjoy one of their plant-based milk shakes, juices, boost shots or infused waters. They have all been formulated to be beneficial for your body and are frankly delicious.

22 KIKI MARKET
Travesía de San Mateo 4
Centro ①
+34 915 027 339
www.kiki-market.com/ wordpress

This store and restaurant are dedicated to eco-friendly and organic food. Meat, fruit, bread and vegetables plus some little luxuries for healthy freaks like spirulina powder, mixed seed powder and super food supplements. The restaurant's menu features plenty of good food for your body and mind including veggie and gluten-free dishes.

23 BIO IN THE BOWL
Zurbano 15
Chamberí ⑤
+34 917 026 302
www.biointhebowl.com

A nice place for a take-out with a few seats to sit down and eat in. Bio in the Bowl packs every dish in recycled glass bowls. These flexitarians also prep a few meat-based dishes but most importantly their food is gluten-free, contains no added sugar and just the right amount of salt.

24 MAMA CAMPO

Trafalgar 22
Chamberí ⑤
+34 914 474 138
www.mamacampo.es

This organic grocery store sells high-quality locally sourced or organic products. The restaurant, Cantina, has a warm and welcoming setting, and will make you feel as if you ended up in a gypsy farmhouse in the countryside with Dutch designer furniture. The food is succulent and made with eco ingredients only. The menu has plenty of traditional, homemade items to choose from.

25 LA MAGDALENA DE PROUST

Regueros 8
Centro ①
+34 914 673 311
www.lamagdalena deproust.com

The equivalent of a concept store but for 100% ecological products only. A supermarket, a cafeteria for breakfast and lunch, with plenty of take out options, homemade bread and cooking classes. The fruits and vegetables are grown in Madrid thanks to a partnership with a local orchard called Riva.

24 MAMA CAMPO

Top 5
V E G G I E
restaurants

---

26 **COPENHAGEN**
Ortega y Gaset 73
Salamanca ③
+34 911 281 800
www.grupo
copenhagen.com

Originally from Valencia. This restaurant looks like a Scandi design restaurant, which is quite different for a veggie restaurant. All the food is also organic, locally sourced and biodynamic. Some of the dishes are suitable for ovolactovegetarians. Creative cuisine with a surprising twist, highly recommended, even for carnivores!

27 **RAYÉN VEGANO**
Lope de Vega 7
Centro ②
+34 675 382 072
www.rayenvegan.com

This adorable little restaurant only serves homemade cuisine. Even the bread is freshly baked onsite every day. No fried or reheated foods here. They serve a daily menu, with plenty of seasonal fare, as to be paired with beers from microbreweries and ecological wines.

28 **SANISSIMO**
Campomanes 5
Centro ②
+34 911 152 546
www.sanissimo.eu/
opera

Sanissimo is probably the healthiest veggie fast-food restaurant in Madrid, with plenty of affordable options on the menu. Their specialties include veggie burgers, wraps and bagels. Some of the more interesting dishes include a creamy eggplant lasagna with tofu and hummus.

29 CRUCINA

Divino Pastor 30
Centro ①
+34 914 453 364
www.crucina.com

Crucina is the first and only raw vegan restaurant in Madrid. This means none of the ingredients are cooked at a temperature above 41°C, ensuring the natural nutrients and enzymes of the vegetable are preserved. They also use several other interesting cooking techniques such as fermentation, marinades and dehydration of the ingredients.

30 IL TAVOLO VERDE

Villalar 6
Salamanca ③
+34 918 051 512
www.iltavoloverde.com

A real hidden secret! At Tavolo Verde, you may be seduced by one of the many antiques and artisan crafts they sell, or decide to spend the rest of the afternoon sipping tea and enjoying a home-made cake or an organic and veggie-friendly lunch. Located in what used to be the workshop of a bronze craftsman. A truly unique setting.

30 IL TAVOLO VERDE

The 5 nicest
TERRACES
to dine alfresco

---

31 BOSCO DE LOBOS

Hortaleza 63
Centro ①
+34 915 249 464
www.encompania
delobos.com/en/
bosco-de-lobos

Hidden in the inner court of the College of Architecture, this Italian restaurant and its terrace offer an intimate and green escape from the concrete streets of the city centre. Whether you are looking for a romantic dinner or a business lunch, the terrace suits both purposes. We also recommend dining inside, in the architects' dining room.

32 EL MIRADOR DEL THYSSEN

Paseo del Prado 8
Centro ②
+34 914 293 984
elmiradordel
thyssen.com

This is the ultimate terrace for an intimate and romantic dinner. Located on the rooftop terrace of the museum's modern wing, the restaurant is only open in July and August and serves classic Mediterranean cuisine. Have an aperitivo at the outdoor bar before dinner.

33 FRIDA

San Gregorio 8
Centro ①
+34 917 048 286
www.fridamadrid.com

In a small square with trees and a single olive tree, Frida's small but cosy terrace really enjoys a tranquil setting. They serve anything from pizza to tuna tataki or a simple toast with delicious Iberico ham. A terrace where you can satisfy your morning or afternoon cravings and take your pick from a nice selection of snacks.

34 NITTY GRITTY

Doctor Fleming 51
Chamartín ⑦
+34 914 347 333
www.nittygritty.es

Located in the heart of the financial district of Madrid, the patio and terrace are beautifully decorated combining retro romantic and modern industrial styles. The food is inspired by the coasts of the Mediterranean and includes some classic Spanish dishes.

35 ARZABÁL REINA SOFIA

Santa Isabel 52
Centro ②
+34 915 286 828
www.arzabal.com

This is the latest addition to the Arzabál food empire. Open from May to the end of October, the terrace transports you to an urban midsummer night's dream. A refreshing place to enjoy a nice selection of classic northern dishes. Their signature grilled fish and meat dishes are only available at their Reina Sofia address.

31 BOSCO DE LOBOS

The 5 best places for
SANDWICHES

---

36 LA GARRIGA
Génova 21
Chamberí ⑤
+34 913 100 540
www.lagarriga
charcuteria.com

La Garriga's reputation is based on more than half a century of history. The shop now also serves tapas and sandwiches and is the perfect stop for a tasty snack at any time of the day. Here you will find the best *sobrasada* and melted cheese sandwich in town.

37 EL PORRÓN CANALLA
Ballesta 2
Centro ①
+34 915 320 604
www.elporron
canalla.com

By bringing back the tradition of sharing a dun of beer and lemonade (Porrón) they also innovate on the sandwich side by shaking up some traditional recipes. The Calamari sandwich is a call back and the veal sandwich with the canalla sauce is a perfect match with the *porrón*.

38 LA CASA TOMADA
San Lorenzo 9
Centro ①
+34 915 138 448

This place serves big sandwiches and we mean really big. The kind of sandwiches that will fill you up for the rest of the day. Roast beef, teriyaki and fried chicken are just a few of the 17 sandwiches you can choose from. The bread is just perfectly soft yet crunchy at the same time.

39 BOQUADILLO DE JAMÓN Y CHAMPAGNE

Menéndez Pelayo 15
Retiro ④
www.bocadillo
dejamon.com

The name says it all: an Iberico ham sandwich with champagne is what you'll find here! Choose from a wide selection of breads and plenty of champagnes by the glass. The interiors are elegant combining wood and brass with light colours and views of Retiro Park.

40 SANGUCHÓN

Hartzenbusch 7
Chamberí ⑤
+34 911 996 145
www.sanguchon.es

Peruvian-style sandwiches served in a small restaurant with only a few bar tables. At Sanguchón, you can experience the essence of Peruvian street food, which consists of a round white bread with juicy and tasty meat and a slightly spicy sauce. Choose from five options, including beef, chicken, veal, pork and pork rib.

37 EL PORRÓN CANALLA

5 places to enjoy
IBERIC HAM

---

41 CINCO JOTAS
Callejón de
Puigcerdà s/n
Salamanca ③
+34 915 754 125
*www.restaurantescin
cojotas.com*

Located at the entrance of the Madrid's busiest street for fine dining. The interior of Cinco Jotas will instantly transport you to an elegant Andalusian estate. They have been making Cinco Jotas ham for centuries and it is considered one of the best in the world. Their restaurant is a demonstration of their 'savoir-faire'.

42 JOSELITO'S
Velázquez 30
Salamanca ③
+34 917 274 762
www.joselito.com

The Velázquez flagship of Joselito is both a shop and a restaurant where you can taste the goods. The distinctive red and black colours of the brand add an elegant touch to the interior of this place, which is open continuously. But here too, all that counts is the ham again, and it really is one of the best hams in the world.

43 LA BOULETTE
AT: MERCADO DE LA PAZ,
STAND 63-68
Entrance: Lagasca 49
Salamanca ③
+34 914 317 725
www.laboulette.com

Located in the food market of La Paz, La Boulette is the favourite deli of the locals in the Salamanca neighbourhood. Selling a wide selection of various parts of the ham, they will gladly advise you what to choose. They can also vacuum-pack your deli meats.

44 LÓPEZ PASCUAL

Corredera Baja de
San Pablo 13
Centro ①
+34 915 228 512
*www.jamonesibericos
madrid.com*

Since 1919, López Pascual has been selling the best selection of ham products, making its shop the oldest in Madrid. For three generations they have been selecting the best hams from Jabuco, Cumbres, Mayores and Guijuelo, making personally sure that the curing process respects tradition.

45 ÁLBORA

Jorge Juan 33
Salamanca ③
+34 917 816 197
*www.restaurante
albora.com*

A great bar to discover the art of Iberico ham and enjoy it in many if not all of its forms as an ingredient in several recipes. Share various dishes in this elegant and minimalist setting. A must try is the trio of Iberico ham, which has been cured since 2011, 2012 and 2013.

41 CINCO JOTAS

5
MADRID CLASSICS
loved by the locals

---

46 **CASA LABRA**
Tetuán 12
Centro ②
+34 915 310 081
www.casalabra.es

Its mythical façade, which dates from 1860, continues to attract Madrileños who enjoy the house specialties, namely cod fritters and cod croquetas. Expect a long queue at lunchtime, as it is the perfect bite to whet your appetite, especially when paired with a nice cold beer.

47 **CASA LUCIO**
Cava Baja 35
Centro ②
+34 913 653 252
www.casalucio.es

A real institution in Madrid which was established by Lucio Blázquez more than 40 years ago. Many celebrities who visited Madrid over the years considered this place a mandatory stop and had their picture taken with Lucio. His renowned eggs and potatoes may have been copied in many of the surrounding restaurants but the original is still the best!

48 LA DOLORES

Plaza Jesús 4
Centro ②
+34 914 292 243

This is the perfect place to enjoy a draft beer and a platter of their homemade potato chips with anchovies in vinegar. While this may sound like a strange mix, be careful because some find it quite addictive. Founded in 1908, La Dolores's facade with its typical tiles tells you exactly what you can expect here: good, cool beer and tapas.

49 CASA PERICO

Ballesta 18
Centro ①
+34 915 328 176
www.casaperico
madrid.es

Also called the house of the spoon, Casa Perico is the place to go for what the Spanish call 'spoon dishes', meaning dishes to be eaten with a spoon. Since 1942, they have been serving lentils on Wednesdays, beans on Thursdays and chickpea soup on Friday. A true castizo restaurant.

50 SAN GINÉS

Pasadizo de
San Gines 5
Centro ②
+34 913 656 546
www.chocolateria
sangines.com

Who said you couldn't enjoy *churros* with chocolate at 3 am the morning? Since 1894, San Ginés has been serving deep fried fritters with strong and thick Spanish-style chocolate. The place is open 24 hours a day and there's always a crowd.

5 restaurants to
EAT AND PARTY
UNTIL 3 AM

---

51 **MARIETA**
Paseo de la
Castellana 44
Salamanca ③
+34 915 757 553
www.marieta
madrid.com

Marieta has an open space for parties. The menu has plenty of interesting variations that will suit everyone including artichokes with Iberico ham, a mini Marieta Kebab or a Beef Wellington that is just perfect. Once the volume is cranked up and the lights are turned down, around 1 am, the party finally starts and the vibe is always amazing.

52 **TATEL**
Paseo de la
Castellana 36
Salamanca ③
+34 911 721 841
www.tatel
restaurants.com

A restaurant and bar, Tatel is an innovative concept that will have you wonder whether you're in New York instead of in Madrid. The 800-square metre place is quite unique, with live music at dinner, a DJ and excellent cocktails. Sponsored by Enrique Iglesias, Rafa Nadal and Pau Gasol, this place is a must-visit.

53 **PERRACHICA**
Eloy Gonzalo 10
Chamberí ⑤
+34 917 377 775
perrachica.com

A 900-square metre space that is entirely dedicated to leisure, from morning until night. In this huge and stylish space that is a blend of colonial, tropical and retro styles, the Larrumba group has once again demonstrated how savvy they are when it comes to entertainment.

54 **JUANITA CRUZ**

Paseo de la
Habana 105
Chamartín ⑦
+34 914 511 776
www.juanitacruz.com

Juanita Cruz is located in an old metro station that has been converted into a restaurant and club, adding a clandestine feel. Mixing influences of English clubs with a funky approach, this is a nice and fun place to go. The menu includes mini bull tail (rabo de toro) burgers or panchitos of cochinita pibil.

55 **POINTER**

Marqués de
la Ensenada 16
Centro ①
+34 910 526 928
pointermadrid.com

Pointer is the newest addition to Madrid's bar/restaurant scene. This 2-storey restaurant offers various ambiances, all clearly influenced by New York's restaurant scene. The menu mixes flavours from the east, the west and Spain. Head downstairs for the party, where everybody is always dancing to the music.

53 PERRACHICA

The 5 latest
HOTSPOTS

---

56 **HABANERA**
Génova 28
Centro ①
+34 917 372 017
*www.habanera
madrid.com*

With the exuberant and elegant look and feel of a colonial patio in La Habana, Habanera is a 900-square metre emporium to the art of gastronomy, where you are bound to have a good time. The menu is a nice mix of Mediterranean and Caribbean. Try the amazing cocktails by master mixologist Carlos Moreno.

57 **AMAZONICO**
Jorge Juan 20
Salamanca ③
+34 915 154 332
*www.restaurante
amazonico.com*

The latest venture of the owners of the excellent Paraguas, Ten con Ten and Quintin exceeds expectations. The interior is absolutely amazing and will transport you to an über-cool restaurant in the middle of the Amazonian forest. Ceviche, *tartar* or *kofta* for starters and choose meat for your main course.

58 **BABELIA**
Callejón de
Puig-cerdà 6
Salamanca ③
+34 918 317 179
*www.babelia
restaurante.com*

Set at one end of the famous Puigcerdá Street, Babelia has a very pleasant terrace and a two-storey restaurant, with an interior design by Madrid in Love. Easy-going menu with classics that never fail. Stay for drinks after dinner, the ambiance is compelling.

59 BIBO

**Paseo de la
Castellana 52
Salamanca ③
+34 918 052 556
*www.grupodanigarcia.
com/bibo-madrid***

Everybody knows Chef Dani Garcia.
This is the Madrid version of his famous
Marbella restaurant at the Puente Romano
hotel. This is a more cosmopolitan,
affordable version of his supreme cuisine,
which is inspired by Andalucia. The
interiors are absolutely astonishing!

60 DSTAGE

**Regueros 8
Centro ①
+34 917 021 586
*www.dstage
concept.com***

The name is an acronym of 'Days to
Smell Taste Amaze Grow & Enjoy' and
a good example of the new and genius
generation of Michelin-starred restaurants
(2 stars in the 2017 edition). It's all about
innovation in a relaxed setting with an
industrial touch and concept cuisine.
Latin, Asian and Spanish flavours will
rock and roll your senses.

59 BIBO

5

TRENDY *and*
AFFORDABLE *places*

61 **MAKKILA**
   Núñez de Balboa 75
   Salamanca ③
   +34 917 372 701
   www.makkila.com

Combining Art Deco with wood, interesting lamps and fabrics in earthy shades with Kilim cushions you get an idea of the latest addition to the Makkila project. This cosy 420-square metre restaurant is known for its excellent *pinchos* and *raciones* (sharing platters) such as the tortilla with caramelised onion or the octopus with mashed potatoes.

62 **LAMUCCA**
   Serrano 91
   Salamanca ③
   +34 915 210 000
   www.lamucca
   company.com

The restaurant is usually packed because of its informal yet chic setting, and its wide range of international menu options. It is also open every day of the year, which is nice. Expect a mix of vintage furniture in an industrial setting in a refurbished classic Madrid house.

63 **WHITBY**
   Almagro 22
   Chamberí ⑤
   +34 913 197 088
   www.whitby.es

This is a classic place in Madrid for an easy-going dinner with friends. This little restaurant offers just what you need.Here the food is casual, the music is entertaining and the people are good-looking. Hang around for drinks after dinner!

64 DRAY MARTINA

Argensola 7
Centro ①
+34 910 810 056
www.draymartina.com

This is one of the first and oldest restaurants in Madrid with a vintage and romantic interior. It is also a perfect place for a date night or a night out with the girls. Serves a cosmopolitan menu and is nicely located near bars for after-dinner drinks.

65 LA CONTRASEÑA

Ponzano 6
Chamberí ⑤
+34 911 726 378
www.restaurantela
contrasena.com

Don't be fooled by the entrance and the nice bar. The restaurant behind it is decorated in a modern colonial style. Here you can eat a la carte, order an informal snack, have a drink after work or even enjoy your first drink of the night. Definitely one of the must-go places in the new foodie quarter of the city that is Calle Ponzano.

61 MAKKILA

5

INNOVATIVE

restaurant concepts

---

66 **SALA DE DESPIECE**
Ponzano 11
Chamberí ⑤
+34 917 526 106
*www.academia
deldespiece.com*

The name of the restaurant means the cutting room and is an obvious reference to a butcher shop. Here tools are exhibited on the walls, which are lined with polystyrene boxes. Most of the tapas are finished in front of you or by you. Try the ribeye with tomato and truffle.

67 **BARRA /M**
Libertad 5
Centro ①
+34 916 684 678
*www.barraeme.
pacificogrupo.com*

This is a revolutionary concept where everything happens at the bar. Food is cooked, served and eaten on the angular metal structure. /M is a nondescript project dreamed up by the renowned Peruvian Chef Omar Malpartida. As evening turns into night, you will forget that you actually came for dinner as you swing to the beat of the music.

68 **KULTO**
Ibiza 4
Retiro ④
+34 911 733 053
www.kulto.es

It is difficult to qualify their cuisine, which is very personal with ample references to Andalucian food. Downstairs they serve tapas in an open space with two bars. Upstairs: a cosy and nicely decorated mezzanine for formal dining. Tuna is the main protagonist on the menu.

69 NUBEL

Argumosa 43
Centro ②
+34 915 301 761
www.nubel.es

Located in the impressive Jean Nouvel annexe of the Reina Sofia Museum, which was inaugurated in 2005 and has since 2016 become Nubel. Open from breakfast until 2.30 am, in the morning Nubel's originality does not just lie in its interior design but also in the dinner menu of Javier Muñoz-Calero. Food in its purest form.

70 FLORIDA RETIRO

Paseo de Panamá 1
Retiro ④
+34 918 275 275
www.floridaretiro.com

Located in Retiro Park, this has always been a favourite place for social gatherings since 1814. Nowadays it's a gastronomic complex with various restaurants, tapa bars, terraces and La Sala, which hosts festive dinners and show nights produced by Yllana, the creator of the famous show the Hole.

69 NUBEL

5 great restaurants for
GALICIAN *and* BASQUE
specialities

---

71 TABERNA GAZTELUPE
Comandante
Zorita 32
Tetuán ⑥
+34 915 349 116
gaztelupe.goizeko-
gaztelupe.com

A traditional Basque restaurant with white tablecloths, a traditional interior design, excellent service and superb raw ingredients. Focus on the food, and the outstanding selection of fresh seafood, fish and especially tuna when in season (March to June). They also have a wine list with more than 200 (mainly Spanish) references.

72 ARIMA
Ponzano 51
Chamberí ⑤
+34 911 091 599
www.arimabasque
gastronomy.com

Arima means soul in Basque and refers to the traditions that are handed down from generation to generation. An informal setting, that makes a clean break with the traditional design of the Basque tavern. Arima adds a playful twist to northern classics. Their amazing list of vermuts and cocktails is an incentive to stay a little longer.

73 URKIOLA MENDI
Cristóbal Bordiú 52
Chamberí ⑤
+34 917 555 762
www.urkiolamendi.net

In the past 18 years, they may have moved a few times, but the quality and passion has remained the same. The team hails from Bilbao and their talent is Bacalao (cod fish). With only seven tables, the service is very personal. Try one of their homemade desserts.

74 O'PAZO

Reina Mercedes 20
Tetuán ⑥
+34 915 532 333
www.opazo.es

Since 1981, O'pazo has been serving the best seafood and fish to the people of Madrid. In a very elegant setting that is miles away from the cliché of a Galician seafood restaurant, you can enjoy fantastic turbot or great flounder. Have a nice assortment of shellfish including sea urchins and percebes as a starter.

75 CANNIBAL RAW BAR

Almirante 12
Centro ①
+34 910 268 794
www.cannibalrawbar.es

The original restaurant is located in la Coruña in Galicia. But no worries, the Madrid restaurant offers the exact same menu and an even nicer ambiance. Cannibal Raw Bar is a new take on Galician cuisine, placing emphasis on seafood carpaccio and ceviches.

74 O'PAZO

5 restaurants for
CENTRAL and LATIN AMERICAN FOOD

76 **A&G MADRID**
Ayala 27
Salamanca ③
+34 917 026 262
www.aygmadrid.com

Astrid and Gaston, since 2014 the precursors of Peruvian Haute Cuisine, have put Chef Percy Álvaro in charge of their Madrid restaurant. With a super minimalist interior and endless respect for the 500-year tradition of Peruvian cuisine, A&G Madrid is a legend. *Causas*, seafood *chaufa* and the ceviche are excellent. Don't forget to sample the Pisco Sour.

77 **TIRADITO & PISCO BAR**
Conde Duque 13
Centro ①
+34 915 417 876
www.tiradito.es

The first restaurant of Chef Omar Malpartida displays the wealth and variety of Peruvian cuisine with a wide variety of products from the Amazon, the sea and its fields. The menu only lists 12 dishes, which change depending on the season and are subject to product availability. Good cocktails with home macerated *piscos*.

78 LA LUPITA

Conde de Xiquena 10
Centro ①
+34 911 526 565
www.lalupita.es

Coming straight from Mexico D.F., in Madrid the owners finally sell real tacos that you can eat with two fingers. A taqueria with a relaxed and easy-going ambiance in a contemporary styled restaurant. The tortillas are homemade, with grilled ingredients. A favourite is the tacos del Pastor. Pair it with a refreshing Margarita.

79 LA CANDELITA

Barquillo 30
Centro ①
+34 915 238 553
www.lacandelita.es

Even though this is officially a Venezuelan restaurant, the style is more Latin American and that includes the ingredients, spices and techniques from various Latin American regions. There is even a distinct Japanese feel to their cuisine. In this free-spirited restaurant, food is all about enjoyment. You will have a good time at this lively place.

80 PUNTO MX

General Pardiñas 40-B
Salamanca ③
+34 914 022 226
www.puntomx.es

With one Michelin star, Punto MX is a reference for outstanding Mexican cuisine, in Madrid but also in Europe. The chef takes a modern approach, reinventing traditional recipes and creating unique dishes. The interiors are simple and blend nicely with what's on your plate. Don't forget the mezcalLab cocktail bar on the first floor.

The 5 best
TABERNAS
for tapas and more

---

81 **LA CASTELA**

Doctor Castelo 22
Retiro ④
+34 915 735 590
www.restaurante
lacastela.com

Divided into two areas with the bar at the entrance and a quiet restaurant in the backroom, la Castela is always jam-packed. But you'll want to stay at the bar for a beer or a glass of wine, paired with a nice selection of tapas. Or why not share a dish from their menu? The *milhojas de ventresca* (layered red pepper and tuna salad) is a must.

82 **TASCA CELSO Y MANOLO**

Libertad 1
Centro ①
+34 91 531 80 79
www.celsoymanola.es

After refurbishing but maintaining the typical bar of a respectable taberna and the original tile floor, Celso y Manolo now offers tapas and small dishes based on traditional Spanish flavours. Huesca tomatoes, *rabas* de Santander (fried squid) or *empanadillas* of tuna are just of few of their recipes that never go out of fashion.

83 LA RAQUETISTA

Doctor Castelo 19
Retiro ④
+34 918 311 842
www.laraquetista.com

The Retiro neighbourhood and Calle Ponzano are the up-and-coming gastronomic bastions of Madrid. La Raquetista is a good example of the dedication and work that goes into offering outstanding cuisine at a very reasonable price. The ambiance in the bar is always nice. Try a few dishes from the menu along with their tapas.

84 LA CARMENCITA

Libertad 16
Centro ①
+34 915 310 911
*www.taberna
lacarmencita.es*

La Carmencita is the second oldest taberna in Madrid (1854) and has served famous guests such as Pablo Neruda. Although renovated, everything has been kept intact, from the polychrome tiles to the tin and the wood bar at the entrance (the property was listed as a monument by the City Council).

85 TABERNA PEDRAZA

Ibiza 38
Retiro ④
+34 910 327 200
*www.taberna
pedraza.com*

Carmen, the wife, is in charge of the kitchen while her husband, Ramón, manages the front of the house. The interior is a subtle revival of the seventies by the famous interior designer Lázaro Rosa Violán. On the menu: creamy croquetas, classic dishes and their famous liquid tortilla.

5

FUSION RESTAURANTS

worth a visit

---

86 **BISTRONOMIKA**
Santa María 39
Centro ②
+34 911 386 298
*www.bistro
nomika.com*

This contemporary bistro serves global cuisine. Asian and Latin flavours, mixed with only the best nationally sourced ingredients. 'We Cook the Sea' is their motto. Wild line-caught fish from Galicia, Asturias, Cádiz or the Canary Islands are always on the menu.

87 **SASHA BOOM**
Raimundo Fernán-
dez Villaverde 26
Chamberí ⑤
+34 911 995 010
*www.restaurante
sashaboom.com*

At Sasha Boom, the Middle East has fused with the Mediterranean with special attention to Lebanese and Greek cuisine. The menu is not extensive but the 20 dishes on it are pretty powerful. The terrace is open during summer and winter, which, along with the nice cocktails, is why you'll find so much of the ACZA business clientele for after work drinks and dinner.

88 **BACIRA**
Castillo 16
Chamberí ⑤
+34 918 664 030
www.bacira.es

The new kid on the block in the city, which means booking in advance. With an informal setting, affordable prices and the passionate work of three friends, Bacira soon emerged with a fusion cuisine everyone understands. The Mediterranean cuisine, with fascinating hints of Asia, leaves a fresh, spicy and tart taste in our mouth.

---

89 CHIFA

Modesto Lafuente 64
Chamberí ⑤
+34 915 347 566

Chifa is an easy-going, small restaurant with seating for 25 people including at the bar. The interior is ultra-minimalist with a 50s look and feel and perfect for its purpose as an eatery. China and Latin America are fused in dishes such as the 'Causa a la Hamanako' or the 'Pekingese chaufa rice'.

90 NO NAME

Alberto Aguilera 5
Centro ①
+34 670 088 427
www.nonamebar.es

This restaurant with its eclectic interior, graffiti, DJ and cocktails has a good night in store for you. It is called 'No Name' because they never found the right name for their restaurant! Sushi, rolls and Nigiris are the stars of their Japanese fusion cuisine but the Wayega burger is infused with a small touch of Spain.

87 SASHA BOOM

5 places for your
AFTERNOON SUGAR KICK

---

91 **MOTTEAU**
San Pedro 9
Centro ②
+34 910 523 201

Pastries made with respect for Juan Manuel's French ancestors from Normandy, mixed with an American influence. The result: a fantastic carrot cake, tremendous brownies and a soft cheesecake. On the French side, you can choose between a delicate lemon and *meringue* tart, the famous Tarte Tatin or a croissant that is made to perfection.

92 **LA MEJOR TARTA DE CHOCOLATE DEL MUNDO**
Alcalá 89
Salamanca ③
+34 915 775 008
www.lamejortarta chocolatedelmundo.com

Many birthdays have been celebrated with the best chocolate cake in the world. Created by Portuguese chef Carlos Braz Lopes, his chocolate cakes have seduced plenty of people, with shops around the world, including in Australia, France, Angola and Brazil. What makes his chocolate so interesting is its strong chocolate taste and very digest chocolate merengue.

93 LA DUQUESITA

Fernando VI 2
Centro ①
+34 913 080 231
www.laduquesita.es

In 1914, La Duquesita opened in Fernando VI Street, marking the start of the history of this emblematic Madrid bakery. Since 2016, the chocolate artisan and pastry chef Oriol Balaguer has been in charge of this old lady, choosing to maintain the tradition. Creativity and innovation prime in the elaboration of his deserts, chocolates and sweets.

94 ROCAMBOLESC

Serrano 52
Salamanca ③
+34 915 765 234
www.rocambolesc.com

Located on the top floor of the Corte Inglés department store in their gastronomic project Gourmet Experience, this ice cream parlour is the work of the Roca family. Infused with the incredibly creative cuisine of the Rocas, their ice cream is a true gastronomic experience. Try any of the suggestions or challenge their art by composing your own ice cream.

95 LOLO POLO

Léon 30
Centro ②
+34 910 516 764
www.lolopolosarte
sanos.es

In this ice cream parlour in Malasaña, the popsicles are homemade, with no additives, no colouring, very little sugar and only fresh seasonal fruits. Think it sounds too healthy to be good? Well, think again. You'll be pleasantly surprised by some of their original mixes such as cucumber and lime or raspberry and Jamaica water.

5 of the best
DELIS
in town

---

96 **EMBASSY**
Paseo de la
Castellana 12
Salamanca ③
+34 914 359 480
www.embassy.es

Founded in 1931 by Irish Margarita K. Taylor, Embassy soon became famous for its lemon tart and pastries. Today it is one of the most prestigious delis with a wide range of products ranging from champagnes, foie gras, caviar, homemade canapés, cooked dishes, cheese and charcuterie.

97 **LA MELGUIZA**
Santiago 12
Centro ②
+34 915 479 323
www.lamelguiza.es

Near San Miguel market, this small and minimalist deli has chosen to sell a treasure that was once more experience than gold per ounce, namely saffron. At 10 euros per gram, this Spanish gold can be bought raw or used in a variety of products such as olive oil, chocolates or sausages.

98 **CRISTINA ORIA**
Conde de Aranda 6
Salamanca ③
+34 639 275 761
www.cristinaoria.com

After studying in Paris at the Cordon Bleu, Cristina opened her own catering and gourmet shop. In 2011, at the age of 27, she won the 1st prize at Madrid Fusión with her foie gras mi-cuit and gelatine of 3 Sauternes wines, which is her star product and is considered to be the best foie gras in the world (available in the shop).

99 MANTEQUERIA BRAVO

Ayala 24
Salamanca ③
+34 915 758 072
www.bravo1931.com

Since 1931, this familiar corner shop has evolved to become a reference in Madrid when you are searching for international products such as sauces, teas, preserves or mortadella from Bologna. They have a wide range of products, and you can find any preserved or dried ingredient that you need for most classic dishes here.

100 TIENDA PONCELET

Argensola 27
Centro ①
+34 913 080 221
www.poncelet.es

Madrid's cheese heaven. The shop design is interesting and different from a classic cheese counter. Here cheese is presented like jewellery, and organised by region. Name any cheese and they are bound to have it. They sell 280 types in all! Their restaurant Cheese Bar at José Abascal 61 serves almost all of them.

99 MANTEQUERIA BRAVO

The 5 best
BAKERIES

---

101 PANIC

Conde Duque 13
Centro ①
+34 910 862 201

This artisan and ecologic bakery is one of the sourdough bread trendsetters in Madrid. Selling six types of bread, all simple and straightforward, Panic believes in letting the flavour of the bread be the star. So they don't add any nuts, grains, fruits or other ingredients.

102 EL HORNO DE BABETTE

Ayala 79
Salamanca ③
+34 918 282 096
www.elhorno debabette.com

This originally started out as a cooking school where Beatriz was teaching her students how to make real bread. But it was such a success that she now has four bakeries, including one that also sells cooking utensils. Her latest venture in Ayala also serves cheese.

103 LEVADURA MADRE

Diego de León 61
Salamanca ③
+34 914 014 203
www.levadura madre.es

Sourdough is made from flour and water, which starts to ferment spontaneously. This starter forces Levadura Madre to work slowly, to knead the dough one day, to let it ferment during the night and to shape the bread the next day. During those 24 hours, the flavours develop in the dough, which is why they bake some of the best breads in town here.

104 CELICIOSO

Barquillo 19
Centro ①
+34 915 318 887
www.celicioso.com

Part of the beautiful Only You boutique hotel, Celicioso is the first 100% gluten-free bakery in Madrid. The aim is to offer a wide range of freshly-baked, gluten-free pastries that can be enjoyed by anyone: cakes, cupcakes, cookies, chocolates, breads and savoury breads to eat in or take out.

105 QUADRA PANIS

Lepanto 4
Centro ②
+34 913 624 260
www.quadrapanis.com

Nuncio, the Italian founder of Quadra Panis, is so active that he cannot keep his hands still and that is why he kneads up to 180 different types of authentic bread every day. He named his bakery after the white bread that the patricians ate every day in ancient Rome. Enjoy!

HEAD

HEART

TAIL

16-10-1793

MACERA

70 PLACES
FOR A DRINK

5 places for **COFFEE** or **TEA** —————— 70

5 wonderful **BOOKSHOP CAFES** —————— 72

5 amazing **ROOFTOP BARS** —————— 74

The 5 best **SPEAKEASY COCKTAIL BARS**—— 76

5 buzzing **AFTER WORK BARS** —————— 79

5 clubs to **PARTY UNTIL DAWN** —————— 81

5 **CERVECERÍAS** to enjoy a good beer —————— 83

5 of the best **WINE BARS** —————— 85

5 places to enjoy **A GLASS OF VERMUT** —————— 87

5 of the most **AUTHENTIC BARS** in Madrid—————— 90

The 5 best **GIN & TONIC** cafes—————— 92

The 5 places to hang out in **MALASAÑA** —————— 94

5 **LGBT BARS** in Chueca—————— 96

5 cool **HIPSTER BARS** —————— 98

5 places for
COFFEE *or* TEA

---

106 TOMA CAFÉ
La Palma 49
Centro ①
+34 917 025 620
www.tomacafe.es

With bikes parked out front and inside, you already know that this cool coffee shop is a fave with hipsters. Your assumption is confirmed once you enter and inhale the strong flavour of coffee and see the recycled vintage furniture. The barista makes an excellent espresso.

107 SALON DES FLEURS
Guzmán el Bueno 106
Chamberí ⑤
+34 915 352 348
www.salondesfleurs.es

At first glance, this place looks like a flower shop but it has much more to offer. Inside you will discover an über-cosy and welcoming British tearoom. A romantic place to enjoy teas such as green tea with champagne and strawberries and a slice of their homemade cakes. The shabby chic decorative objects are almost all for sale.

108 VAILIMA
Salustiano Olózaga 18
Salamanca ③
+34 913 090 955
www.vailima.es

Conceived as a tearoom, Vailima has more than 150 varieties of tea from around the world. The romantic style of a Parisian bistro mixed with checkerboard floors, exposed brick walls and cast iron furniture makes this the perfect place for a nice afternoon break. Try one of the many homemade cakes or croissants.

109 PUM PUM CAFÉ

Tribulete 6
Centro ②
+34 911 999 854
www.pumpumcafe.com

The former butcher shop has become a vegetarian coffee shop. Their coffee is ecological, freshly-roasted and grounded by a small Madrid producer and the milk is brought in fresh from the Sierra of Madrid. Exposed brick walls and vintage school chairs add to the discreet charm of this place.

110 HANSO CAFÉ

Pez 20
Centro ①
+34 911 375 429

The latest addition to Madrid's coffee bars is the project of 3 Chinese friends and entrepreneurs. With superb coffees from Nicaragua, Kenya, Colombia or Ethiopia and a La Marzocco their coffees are simply excellent. A perfect mix of Spanish and Chinese culture in an industrial space with tiles and open window seating.

5 wonderful
BOOKSHOP CAFES

---

111 SWINTON AND GRANT
Miguel Servet 21
Centro ②
+34 914 496 128
www.planet.
swintonandgrant.com

Swinton is the gallery dedicated to contemporary art and Grant is the bookstore for books on urban art, contemporary art, comics and graphic novels. You will find them both in an industrial building in Lavapies district. The café on the ground floor is called 'Cuiadando Grant'.

112 TIPOS INFAMES
San Joaquín 3
Centro ①
+34 915 228 939
www.tiposinfames.com

The 'Infamous Types' are Alfonso, Gonzalo and Francisco. Their bookstore specialises in independent literature and organises various activities including exhibitions, tastings and reading sessions. Coffee and wine are firm favourites in this café, with tables arranged among the bookshelves.

113 LA FABRICA
Alameda 9
Centro ②
+34 912 985 523
www.lafabrica.com

This multidisciplinary space has a café, a gift shop with a great selection of art books and a photography gallery. Ever since it opened in 1995, La Fabrica has developed cultural projects that add value to our society. Disciplines they favour for their projects, are photography and the visual arts, literature, cinema, music and the performing arts.

114 OCHO Y MEDIO LIBROS DE CINÉ

**Martín de
los Heros 11
Centro** ①
+34 915 590 628

The specialist for cinema buffs with books, scripts, journals and essays. There are two cafes onsite: Via Margutta and El Gatopardo. In summer, they also have a great terrace in Calle Martín. The Italian *tramezzini* sandwiches are a must-eat at Via Margutta.

115 LA CENTRAL – EL BISTRÓ

**Postigo de
San Martín 8
Centro** ②
+34 917 909 970
www.lacentral.com

Located in a 1200-square metre palace, La Central has an inventory of more than 70.000 volumes and specialises in philosophy, history, social sciences and literature. Other occupants of this 3-storey building include a café-restaurant (El Bistró) and a cocktail bar (El Garito). They also host various cultural activities.

115 LA CENTRAL – EL BISTRO

5 amazing
ROOFTOP
bars

---

116 **DEAR HOTEL – NICE TO MEET YOU**

Gran Vía 80
Centro ①
+34 638 908 559
www.dearhotel
madrid.com

On the 14th floor of the Dear hotel, this is the terrace to watch the sunset. With views of Plaza de España, Casa de Campo and all the way to the Sierra, 'Nice to meet you' is an amazing urban garden. The restaurant and cocktail bar are open to the public.

117 **THE PRINCIPAL – TERRAZA**

Marqués de
Valdeiglesias 1
Centro ①
+34 915 218 743
www.theprincipal
madridhotel.com

A cosmopolitan and elegant terrace with olive and cypress trees, white marble and forged iron tables and a stylish red fabric for their parasols. With dramatic views of Gran Vía and the Metropolis building, this is the ideal setting for either a sunset or an after-dinner drink. Good cocktails and great music to chill out to.

118 **TERRAZA SUECIA**

Marqués de Casa
Riera 4
Centro ②
+34 912 000 570
www.nh-hoteles.es

This attic with two heights offers unparalleled views over the roofs of the capital. Its warm and super cosy interior makes you feel as if you are in an open air tropical living room: light pink sofas full of fluffy cushions and tables covered in colourful tiles with plenty of greenery. Great cocktails.

119 **SALVADOR BACHILLER**

Montera 37
Centro ②
+34 915 323 399
www.jardindesalvador
bachiller.com

The contentious Calle Montera, which joins Gran Vía to Sol, has had a drastic upgrade in recent years. Halfway this street, you will find Salvador Bachiller's shop, the place for bags and luggage. On the top floor, you will discover a hidden oasis with a terrace full of plants and a peaceful backdrop to enjoy an afternoon tea and sweet snack.

120 **CÍRCULO DE BELLAS ARTES**

Alcalá 42
Centro ②
+34 915 301 761
www.circulobellas
artes.com

This is the only rooftop terrace with a 360° view of Madrid. Minerva, the Roman goddess of wisdom and art, sits atop the building, which rises 56 metres above Alcalá Street. The restaurant and cocktail bar of Javier Muños Calero offers casual cuisine which you can enjoy under the stars.

118 TERRAZA SUECIA

The 5 best
SPEAKEASY
COCKTAIL BARS

---

121 THE DASH
Murillo 5
Chamberí ⑤
+34 687 949 064
www.thedash.es

The Dash, which means a beat or a pinch in bartenders' slang, is a great idea, if you like classic cocktails with a twist. A small lounge, with a spectacular seventies-style bar, low tables, faint lighting and good background music make this a great option for drinks before or after dinner.

122 SALMÓN GURÚ
Echegaray 21
Centro ②
+34 910 006 185

Cocktail lovers in Madrid all know Diego Cabrera. The menu of his speakeasy contains 25 classics, new creations, alcohol-free cocktails and great champagne cocktails. The place has a super funky interior, with hints of the eighties and sixties New York. The underground room offers limited editions as well as brands that are no longer produced or from closed down distilleries.

123 1862 DRY BAR

Pez 27
Centro ⓘ
+34 609 531 151

The meeting point of the most famous mixologists. 1826 Dry Bar is the most prominent cocktail bar in Madrid. 1826 has two meanings. On the one hand, it was the year in which the building was built. At the same time, it was also the year in which the first ever book on cocktails was published. The atmosphere is great and relaxed.

124 V MANNEKEN

Marqués de
Santa Ana 30
Centro ⓘ
+34 615 642 480

During daytime, the doors are open for fans of antiques and restored furniture. At 5 in the afternoon, this tiny cocktail bar opens. It has a menu of 40 classic and popular cocktails from the twenties, thirties and forties, such as the Dry Martini or the Tom Collins. You'll feel as if you are spending the night in the living room of a decadent aristocrat.

125 MACERA

San Mateo 21
Centro ⓘ
+34 910 115 810
www.maceradrinks.com

How to be a cocktail innovator? Macera does this by creating its own distillates from alcohol such as gin, whiskey, rum, vodka and martini and then macerating them with seasonal fruits (red fruits, apples, jalapeño, lime) and spices (cilantro, cardamom or even olives). Their creations are unique.

125 **MACERA**

127 **ULTRAMARINOS QUINTIN**

5 buzzing
AFTER WORK BARS

———

126 **LATERAL CASTELLANA**
Paseo de la
Castellana 42
Salamanca ③
+34 915 752 553
www.lateral.com

Located near the main bank and lawyers' offices in the Serrano and Castellana areas, Lateral still attracts a varied crowd. Their terrace is the meeting point weather permitting. They have a nice selection of tapas and sharing platters as well as wine by the glass, beers and cocktails.

127 **ULTRAMARINOS QUINTIN**
Jorge Juan 17
Salamanca ③
+34 917 864 624
www.ultramarinos quintin.es

Conceived as a bar, restaurant and deli/grocery shop, Quintin is always buzzing from morning till night. Located in the chic Jorge Juan gastronomic district, the third project of the powerful gastronomic couple Sandro and Marta is once again a hit. You'll often run into famous locals and socialites who are having a drink at the bar, which extends out onto the street when crowded.

128 OTTO

**Paseo de la
Castellana 8
Salamanca ③
+34 917 810 928
*www.ottomadrid.com***

After work is here on this summer terrace in the shadows of the trees on Castellana. This very chic Italian restaurant has a very comfortable terrace, where you can enjoy one of their cocktails, a glass of wine or champagne. Pair this with some Italian antipasti and you are set for a good start to the evening.

129 EL PELICANO

**Capitán Haya 43
Tetuán ⑥
+34 912 031 974
*www.elpelicano
madrid.com***

El Pelícano is an amazing restaurant and bar in the Meliá Castilla Hotel, in Cuzco, Madrid's core business and financial district. The space is sophisticated and comfortable with a spectacular terrace, that has been designed like a beach club. A good place to network and have a business lunch.

130 CASA AMERICA – CIEN LLAVES

**Paseo de Recoletos 2
Salamanca ③
+34 915 775 955
*www.cienllaves.com***

Open from May till October, the terrace is hidden in the garden of Casa de America. Enter from Paso de Recoletos and walk out onto a rather large wooden terrace with a bar and a lounge area. A nice urban oasis to withdraw to after a long day of work.

5 *clubs to*
PARTY UNTIL DAWN

---

131 MAMITA
Recoletos 23
Salamanca ③
+34 914 314 956
www.mamita
taqueria.com

This is actually a taquería that serves Mexican food and nice margaritas. But the fun really starts after the dinner service as you walk through the bathroom and through another secret door only to find yourself in the club. Book a table or try to get on the guest list, otherwise it can be quite tricky to get in.

132 CHA CHÁ THE CLUB
Cedaceros 7
Centro ②
www.chacha.es

The most secret and private club on the underground scene of Madrid with exclusive Friday night sessions. They are part of the Re-Movida movement of the city and the über-creative musical scene. You can only get in if you are on the list and must comply with the private club's rules. Located in a 20th-century theatre.

133 SIROCO
San Dimas 3
Centro ①
+34 915 933 070
www.siroco.es

The reference on the Spanish music scene for over 25 years. The lounge is on the street level and the club is in the cellar. Siroco has a powerful sound system that is especially designed for DJs and music sessions. They have the most cutting-edge electro sessions in town.

134 GRAF

María de Molina 50
Chamberí ⑤
+34 911 697 577
www.madrilux.com/en/
clubs/graf-madrid

The young and beautiful crowd of Madrid spend their night dancing to the rhythm of commercial electro hits here. Has everything that you'd expect from a top club: VIP tables, a long queue outside, upmarket dressing, which is why it attracts the youthful elite of Madrid. A place to dance, chat, flirt and have fun.

135 FORTUNY

Fortuny 34
Salamanca ③
+34 913 192 651
www.fortuny
restaurantclub.com

Located in a private mansion, Fortuny is a restaurant on the first floor and a club. This is a traditional club where you go for a drink and maybe take a few steps on the dance floor. As their entertainment is aimed at the 30+ clientele, their big attraction in summer is their beautiful courtyard garden.

5

CERVECERÍAS

to enjoy a good beer

---

136 LA FABRICA DE MARAVILLAS

Valverde 29
Centro ①
+34 915 218 753
www.fmaravillas.com

A craft brewery that has developed a nice selection of beers. Taste them on-site. The brewery is separated from the bar by a glass window. Thanks to the concept of the English 'Brewpub', La fabrica de Maravillas is a place for real beer lovers.

137 MADRIZ HOP REPUBLIC

Cardenal Cisneros 21
Chamberí ⑤
+34 617 792 577
www.cervezas
madriz.com

A nice little place dedicated to craft beers and gourmet burgers. With 8 beers on tap, they have a nice selection. Six of the beers are brewed on-site, while the other two come from an other microbrewery in Madrid or the nearby regions.
A meeting point for those who love Madriz Beer and everything it stands for.

138 LA TAPE

San Bernardo 88
Centro ①
+34 915 930 422
www.latape.com

This is one of the first cervecerías in Madrid to challenge the local bars with beers from the five continents. The beer bar on the street level has three Spanish and three foreign beers on tap, and a seventh that is hand-cranked, designed to pour an English-style beer, by pressure only, without CO_2.

139 BAR MARTIN

Menéndez Pelayo 17
Retiro ④
+34 915 731 167

The third generation of the Jiménez family now runs the bar. Nothing has changed since it was founded in 1940. Have a classic mahou beer with an *empanada*. Drinks come with free tapas (as they should in Spain). On sunny days, the place is packed for the aperitivo before the traditional weekend lunches.

140 CERVECERÍA SANTA BARBARA

Plaza de Santa
Barbara 8
Centro ①
+34 913 190 449
www.cerveceria
santabarbara.com

Since 1815, Santa Barbara brewery has been considered legendary because of its beer. The waiters with their unmistakable white jacket and red shoulder pads are part of the history, some of them have been waiting tables here for various decades. The place has been a meeting point of intellectuals, students and politicians since 1950.

140 CERVECERÍA SANTA BARBARA

5 of the best
WINE BARS

141 VINO Y COMPAÑIA
Plaza de Olavide 5
Chamberí ⑤
+34 91 444 1278
www.vinoycompania.
blogspot.com

A wine shop with almost 800 wines from all corners of the world as well as cavas and champagne. They organise wine tastings every Friday at 9 pm, calling this their 'Wine Friday'. You'll spend two hours tasting six different wines (white, bubbly and red) in a master class. For only 25 euros per person.

142 THE HACIENDA WAREHOUSE
María de Molina 25
Chamartín ⑦
+34 914 365 922
www.the-haciendas.
com/zoritas-kitchen/
madrid.php

Located in a palace, Warehouse occupies the lower floor and garden. Their simple and elegant style brings the farm to the table. Wine is the protagonist here as are the products from their Organic Farm called Hacienda Zorita. The wines are from Madrid, Andalusia, Rioja, Ribera del Duero and France.

143 ANGELITA
Reina 4
Centro ①
+34 915 216 678
www.madrid-
angelita.es

This wine bar, in the centre of Madrid, with the most extensive selection of wine by the glass (25) and the biggest selection of wine by the bottle, has a cellar with 500 wines from around the world. They also serve wines from small producers and a wide selection of Burgundy wines.

144 LAVINIA

**José Ortega y
Gasset 16
Salamanca ③
+34 914 260 599**
www.lavinia.es

Lavinia is probably the biggest wine retailer in Spain. They also have a wine bar and restaurant inside their huge wine shop, which serves a nice tasting menu called the Routes (rutas). You will taste four to five wines and discover regions, grapes and types of wine such as wines from Jerez, or Shiraz and Pinot Noir, wines from Rioja, which is renowned for its Spanish whites.

145 EL QUINTO VINO

**Hernani 48
Tetuán ⑥
+34 915 536 600**
www.elquintovino.com

Head to the bar of this restaurant for a glass of wine with a few tapas. They always have a selection of 10 to 12 wines by the glass. At the bar, they offer smaller versions of the dishes on the menu. Very friendly and nice service.

143 ANGELITA

5 places to enjoy a
GLASS OF VERMUT

___

146 BODEGA DE LA ARDOSA

Colón 13
Centro ①
+34 915 214 979
www.laardosa.es

One of the original 36 bodegas that were founded since 1892, la Ardosa in Colón, where the vermouth is on tap, is one of the few that are still in operation and the most famous one with its red facade. The tradition of the (wine)red colour of the taverns goes back to the middle of the 19th century, when they were painted this colour so that most of the (illiterate) population would be able to identify the taverns.

147 BODEGAS RICLA

Cuchilleros 6
Centro ②
+34 913 652 069

Founded in 1863, this small bar has no place to sit. It does, however, have two beautiful bars decorated with tiles and the walls are lined with beautiful jars and bottles of wine. Here you should have an Yzaguirre Vermouth. The *cecina* (thin slices of cured venison) is also worth a try.

148 ALIPIO RAMOS

Ponzano 30
Chamberí ⑤
+34 914 414 961
www.restaurante
alipioramos.es

Alipio Ramos was founded in 1916, and has ever since sold wine and liquor in bulk. Decorated with old objects that bear witness to its history, such as old barrels of schnapps, a cash register, bottles and a board with the classification of the 1st and 2nd division football teams. A place for a casual weekend vermouth.

149 STOP MADRID

Hortaleza 11
Centro ①
+34 915 218 887
www.stopmadrid.es

Originally opened as a ham and deli store in 1929, this place has succeeded in retaining its original appearance. The Marmol bars are stunning. Order a Miró Vermouth with a few tapas (check the blackboard for what's available).

150 ANGEL SIERRA

Gravina 11
Centro ①
+34 915 310 126

Located next to Chueca Square, this tavern, which was established in 1917, attracts a young crowd, especially around tapa time. A nice place for a glass of Reus Vermouth with pickled tuna and anchovies. In the second room, there is an interesting old wine cellar, with objects from the past and a nice collection of vintage vermouth bottles.

5 of the most
AUTHENTIC BARS
in Madrid

---

151 MUSEO CHICOTE

Gran Vía 12
Centro ⓘ
+34 915 326 737
www.grupomercado
delareina.com/museo-
chicote

This is probably the most mythical bar in the history of Madrid. Originally named Bar Chicote, after its founder Perico Chicote, the barman of the Ritz. In 1931, he opened his own place. Because of his collection of more than 20.000 bottles, he renamed his bar Museum Chicote. Hemingway, Onassis, Loren, Hayworth, Sinatra, Gardner and Peck all frequented this bar.

152 BAR COCK

Reina 16
Centro ⓘ
+34 915 322 826
www.barcock.com

In 1921, a gentleman by the name of Emilio Saracho opened this bar, with a bartender called Perico Chicote (who bought the bar in 1945). Feels like an English club with dark curtains, elegant leather sofas and a marble fireplace. The name might confuse English speakers, but it was intended to be a play on the word Cock-tail.

153 DRY MARTINI

Hermosilla 2
Salamanca ③
+34 914 316 700
www.drymartini
org.com

Located in the Gran Melía Fénix, Dry Martini is the bar of the national cocktail Master Javier de las Muelas. Based on the same concept as the original bar in Barcelona, his Dry Martinis are innovative or served in their most traditional version.

154 JOSÉ ALFREDO

Silva 22
Centro ①
+34 915 214 960
www.josealfredo
bar.com

More than 10 years ago, this place was one of the first in town to serve premium liquors and pave the way for the new and innovative cocktail scene in Madrid. Its green sofas still attract the local crowd and José Alfredo continues to be a reference. Jazz, rhythm & blues and lounge soul in the background.

155 TONI2

Almirante 9
Centro ①
+34 915 320 011
www.toni2.es

If you like to sing, play the piano and you have nowhere to go at 3 am, Toni2 is your place. A classic bar where all generations, styles and backgrounds mingle and hang out around the grand piano to sing classics in Spanish and in English. Once you are inside there is no turning back. You will have a tremendous time and learn not to judge.

The 5 best
GIN & TONIC
cafes

---

156 KIKEKELLER
**Corredera Baja de
San Pablo 17**
Centro ⓘ
+34 915 228 767
www.kikekeller.com

A funny space that is a really cool furniture store and art gallery during daytime and turns into a speakeasy in the evenings from Thursday to Saturday. The retro-futuristic furniture and design objects create a unique interior. Locals from Triball and artists come here for a chat and a good laugh. Indie-pop music in the background.

157 VÁLGAME DIOS
Augusto Figueroa 43
Centro ⓘ
+34 917 010 341

This is a great restaurant and bar for a casual after dinner G&T. The ambiance is lively and it is usually frequented by a very diverse clientele, including many actors, singers, models, designers and writers. Might be because the owners previously worked in fashion.

158 DEL DIEGO
Reina 12
Centro ⓘ
+34 915 233 106
www.deldiego.com

The waiters in their impeccable white jackets welcome you and escort you to your table. Fernando del Diego, who started out as a barman at the famous Chicote Museum, became a star after opening his own cocktail bar. Yes, it is a cocktail bar, but that means the gin is always of premium quality.

159 LA CASA DEL PEZ

Jesús del Valle 1
Centro ⓘ
+34 674 784 636

Eight years ago, La Casa del Pez opened its doors with the idea of offering premium mixed drinks that are still affordable. And they succeeded in their endeavour. Gins are their specialty, with a selection of 20 brands, starting at 5 euros per drink. The Sting and The Botanical's cost 8 euros.

160 SANTAMARÍA LA COCTELERÍA DE AL LADO

Ballesta 6
Centro ⓘ
+34 911 660 511

Located next to a great sandwich place called El Porrón Canalla, this cocktail bar is renowned for its G&Ts. They keep things simple, as it should be, without any additional ingredients. Going out for drinks in places like Santamaria is and can be affordable, delicious and elegant.

156 **KIKEKELLER**

The 5 places to hang out in
MALASAÑA

---

161 MARTÍNEZ BAR
Barco 4
Centro ⓘ
+34 910 802 683

Triball is one of the upgraded areas in Malasaña and has some of the coolest places to hangout in the city. Martinez used to be a brothel. Since 2011, this very cool vintage industrial bar is the place to go for a refreshing G&T. The antique furniture is original and has been recovered from an old tobacco shop.

162 COCONUT BAR
San Roque 14
Centro ⓘ
+34 651 829 373
www.elcoconutbar.com

The interior is the real attraction here. Tiki-Hawaiian with wicker chairs, plastic palm trees and slate tile flooring, with pieces inspired by American culture from the fifties and sixties, that have been imported from Los Angeles and Las Vegas. A good place for your first drink of the weekend.

163 CORAZÓN
Valverde 44
Centro ⓘ
+34 910 257 896
www.salon corazon.com

The interior is rather traditional, somewhere in between a tavern and an English pub. The place has an electric ambiance with a young and fashionable crowd. This is the place to start the evening and get into the mood for a Malasaña night out.

164 TUPPERWARE

**Corredera Alta
de San Pablo 26
Centro ①
+34 625 523 561
*www.tupperware
club.com***

The decoration includes TVs, Nancy's dressing table, Naranjito ceramics, Lava Lamps and Star Trek dolls. Tupperware is the pop temple of Malasaña. When it first opened 10 years ago, it was considered freaky. Nowadays it is a meeting point for pop-rock, free-spirited minds.

165 CAFÉ MODERNO

**Plaza de las
Comendadoras 1
Centro ①
+34 693 528 169
*www.cafemoderno
madrid.com***

Café Moderno's terrace attracts a cheerful crowd on summer days and nights. Close to Conde Duque, Moderno is one of the few big terraces that remains open in August. Mahou fans will be happy (the only beer brand) and their menu is pretty decent for snacks at lunchtime or in the evening.

162 COCONUT BAR

5
LGBT BARS
in Chueca

---

166 BEARBIE
Plaza de Pedro Zerolo 2
Centro ①
+34 620 812 537

Beard lovers or bearded men, look no further, this is your kind of place. This late night gay club, or dance bar, is popular among bears, cubs and their fans. The venue has two floors and plenty of room to dance. Open on Fridays, Saturdays and Sundays only. The vibe is best after 3 am.

167 OCHOYMEDIO
Barceló 11
Centro ①
www.ochoymedio club.com

A cool indie club for an energy-fuelled party. A crowd of flannel shirts and horn-rimmed glasses dance to pumped up electro mixes of eighties and nineties music. Electro-clash and electro-pop make this place a hipster paradise and super gay friendly.

168 BARBANARAMA
San Bartolomé 8
Centro ①
+34 677 210 164

Here you can listen to pop music with hits such as Venus by the band that inspired the name of the bar: Bananarama. A beer will set you back 1,5 euro and mixed drinks cost 5 euros. The interior has a distinct Miami feel to it, and is inspired by the TV show and destination.

169 DELIRIO

Libertad 28
Centro ⓘ
www.delirio
chueca.com

Delirio is a good place to go on Thursday nights, when many other clubs are closed. It is open from midnight until late or early in the morning, with no cover on weeknights. Delirio also hosts DLRO Live (at Calle de Pelayo 59) on Thursday through Saturday with shows and go-go dancers. Mixed crowd.

170 FULANITA DE TAL

Regueros 9
Centro ⓘ
+34 913 195 069
www.fulanita
detal.com

Since 2004, Fulanita de Tal has been a national reference, as it is associated with a fun and recognised brand for the LGBT community. The bar and concert hall also hosts live shows, including small theatre performances, monologues and concerts. Mainly popular with the lesbian community.

5 cool
HIPSTER BARS

---

171 LA BICICLETA
Plaza de San
Ildefonso 9
Centro ①
+34 915 329 742
*www.labicicleta
cafe.com*

At La Bicicleta, they love bikes, coffee and art in equal measure. This concept bar serves various purposes: freelancers love to work here because of the many facilities, it is a meeting point for bike lovers and a gallery with temporary exhibitions of the work of new artists.

172 GORILA
Corredera Baja
de San Pablo 47
Centro ①
+34 915 228 829

At Gorila you can have breakfast, a beer or a snack. A bar for any time of the day. They have a happy hour with a 2 for 1 deal. Their frozen Mojitos and Daiquiris are outstanding too. The setting is 100% hipster: recycled wood, antique chairs, steel and street art on the walls by Mr Hazelnut.

173 NAIF
San Joaquín 16
Centro ①
+34 910 072 071

The place to go for great burgers and beers. The place has an industrial feel with graffiti on the walls. With manageable burgers, compared to many other places, that believe that the giant burger is the way forward. Try the truffle burger or any of the other ten options.

174 **CAZADOR**
Pozas 7
Centro ①
+34 639 970 916

A place for young creative talent, designers and modern artists with artistic interests who go there to chat quietly, and even meet new people over a beer. The interior is eclectic with tapestries with hunting scenes, animal horns and seventies furniture that was rescued from antiques shops, with metallic finishes and design lamps as an interesting twist.

175 **VACACIONES**
Espíritu Santo 15
Centro ①
+34 911 704 015
*www.vacaciones
bar.com*

Designed to look like a beach hut, its Mediterranean vibe and colourful fabrics will make you feel instantly relaxed. This is definitely a happy place to relax and forget your daily hassles for a few hours. Coffees and sandwiches, Mojitos and cocktails, they have something for every time of the day.

175 VACACIONES

EL PARACAIDISTA

70 PLACES TO SHOP

―――――――――――

5 great CONCEPT STORES ――――――――― 102

5 independent SPANISH FASHION brands ―― 104

The 5 best MEN'S STORES ―――――――― 106

5 multi-brand WOMEN'S FASHION stores ―― 108

5 places for TRENDY FRENCH FASHION ― 110

5 JEWELLERY SHOPS for all budgets ――― 112

5 colourful FLOWER SHOPS ―――――― 114

5 lovely BOOKSTORES to spend hours ―――― 116

5 stylish DESIGNER FURNITURE shops ―― 118

5 shops for ESPADRILLES and
CLASSIC SHOES ―――――――――― 120

The 5 best SHOPPING STREETS ――――― 122

5 cool shops for SUNGLASSES ――――― 125

5 specialised RECORD STORES ―――――― 128

The 5 most interesting VINTAGE SHOPS ――― 130

5 *great*
CONCEPT STORES

176 EL PARACAIDISTA
La Palma 10
Centro ①
+34 914 451 913
www.elparacaidista.es

This place is more than a concept store. Go there for some of the coolest fashion, beauty and design. But remember you can also discover new movies at the movie club, have a drink at the Cuban cocktail bar or enjoy a nice meal on their rooftop terrace. A place where you can spend the entire day, surrounded by good taste.

177 EL MODERNO
Corredera Baja
de San Pablo 19
Centro ①
+34 913 483 994
www.elmoderno.es

Their forte is their beautifully curated selection of small furniture and decorative items by world-famous design brands such as Vitra or smaller artisan brands. They also sell nice jewellery, some toys and books. The open space of the shop will inspire you to change a few elements in your own home sweet home.

178 DO DESIGN
Fernando VI 13
Centro ①
+34 913 106 217
www.dodesign.es

A concept store and art gallery, Do Design invites you to see their selection of design elements, decoration and fashion from the same perspective. The shop's design is pure and simple, showcasing a curated selection of French and Japanese brands. The place to find great gifts.

179 MEET

La Palma 15
Centro ⓘ
+34 914 452 422
www.themeetshop.com

They sell fashion, shoes, bags and a very nice selection of ceramics. Their approach is feminine and delicate like many of the things you will find at Meet. Some of the brands they carry are only sold here such as dusen dusen. Craftsmanship and functionality.

180 AMEN

San Andrés 3
Centro ⓘ
www.amenmadrid.com

Amen is your answer to the globalised fashion industry and the lack of individualised design. In a diaphanous space that used to be a printing shop, the shop offers an eclectic selection of fashion and accessories, for both men and women. In the back room they host art exhibitions, secret concerts and DJ sets.

176 EL PARACAIDISTA

5 independent
SPANISH FASHION
brands

181 MASSCOB
Puigcerdà 2
Salamanca ③
+34 914 358 596
www.store.
masscob.com

Originally from La Coruña in the northern part of Spain, Masscob was launched by Marga Massenet and Jacobo Cobián. Relaxed and romantic clothing for women who appreciate clean cuts and believe in the beauty of simplicity. The high-quality garments speak for themselves.

182 ZUBI DESIGN
Zurbano 22
Chamberí ⑤
+34 619 405 919
www.zubidesign.com

This is the story of two sisters from Madrid, who combined their knowledge and passion to create a unique handbag brand. Clutches, backpacks and handbags are printed with a detailed picture from one of their travels including the GPS coordinates of the location. They also sell very nice accessories to complement your bag.

183 ECOALF
Hortaleza 116
Centro ①
+34 917 374 108
www.ecoalf.com

Ecoalf is 100% Spanish but it is also 100% sustainable. It is probably the only environmentally-friendly fashion brand in the world offering such cool designs. All the fabrics are made from recycled materials such as plastic, fishnet, used tires and cotton. The jacket and waistcoat collection for men and women is especially cool.

184 SCALPERS

Jorge Juan 7
Salamanca ③
+34 915 937 216
www.scalpers.es

Founded in 2007 by Borja Vázquez y Rafael Medina, their success started with a tie. Today the brand whose logo is a skull, dresses Spanish men with a nonchalant elegance. Everything from swimsuits to shoes and suits. Their shirts continue to be a best seller and have been seen on many celebrities.

185 BIOMBO 13

Paseo de
La Habana 87
Chamartín ⑦
+34 911 339 594
www.biombo13.net

While studying fashion, Laura Corsini started sewing basic shirts for herself in a wrinkle-free fabric and customising them. Soon her shirts became the basic all her friends wanted. Today she has two shops in Madrid and also sells her elegant basics online at affordable prices. Her shirts are a must in any woman's wardrobe.

181 MASSCOB

The 5 best
MEN'S STORES

186 MAN 1924
Claudio Coello 23
Salamanca ③
+34 915 776 919
www.man1924.com

Carlos Castillo is the creator and creative director of MAN 1924 and has been named as one of the most elegant men by Scott Schuman of Sartorialist. The tailor specialises in suits and jackets and offers a semi-customised service with a hand-finished service.

187 LANDER URQUIJO
Claudio Coello 65
Salamanca ③
+34 917 374 430
www.landerurquijo.com

Specialising in tailoring, Lander Urquijo showcases his own style by mixing classic style with modern pieces. The founder has extensive experience. He started out at age 16 working for a tailor in Bilbao and later moved to two emblematic men's shops in Madrid: MAN 1924 and Anglomania.

188 EL GANSO
Jorge Juan 15
Salamanca ③
+34 914 358 697
www.elganso.com

Relaxed, stylish and budget-friendly, El Ganso is the latest big Spanish fashion hit. Their style combines preppy American with an alternative twist and a hint of British elegance. 100% made in Europe, El Ganso is an optimist fashion brand.

189 **ANGLOMANIA**

Villanueva 16
Salamanca ③
+34 917 810 765
www.anglomania.es

Since 2002, Anglomania has become the bastion of elegance in Madrid. Two floors dedicated to British men's fashions adapted to the Spanish market. Their tailoring service is renowned for the quality of their fabrics and their attention to detail. The collection has both classic pieces and more modern and funkier styles.

190 **EL 91**

Conde de Xiquena 11
Centro ①
+34 914 488 623
www.el91.com

Established only a few years ago, this project is the result of three generations of tailoring expertise. They are neo-artisans with a new vision of tailoring, where craftsmanship, fabrics and imagination come together to offer unique tailor-made garments. Their work is founded on the principles of geometry, simplicity and movement.

186 MAN 1924

5 multi-brand
WOMEN'S FASHION
stores

---

191 NAC
Hermosilla 34
Salamanca ③
+34 912 302 091
www.nac.es

Paul Smith, The Hip Tee, Bergamot or Twin Set are only a few of the brands they carry. Their collections have a boho-chic and romantic style. A great stop for accessories too. The founder, Nani Vazquéz, combined the first letters of her name and of her children's names to create the brand name.

192 EKSEPTION
Velázquez 28
Salamanca ③
+34 915 774 353
www.ekseption.es

This is probably the most avant-garde luxury fashion shop in Madrid. They are always the first or the only ones to have certain unique styles. Their flagship store is worth a visit. It feels like strolling through an art gallery but with Céline bags and Aquazzura stilettos. You might end up treating yourself to one of their sophisticated fragranced candles.

193 COSETTE
Claudio Coello 58
Salamanca ③
+34 915 772 952
www.cosette.es

Clean-cut, simple lines and a French touch of elegance. The difference is in the detail: a specific fold, a ruffle and a special print. You can book a personalised image advice session on Sundays (followed by a brunch) to find out which colour and shape best matches your body and personality.

194 PEZ

Regueros 15
Centro ⓘ
+34 913 106 677
www.pez-pez.es

Beautifully set in a 300-square metre renovated military pharmacy, Pez has been Madrid's trendsetters' favourite stop on their shopping route since 2004. With an effortlessly chic style, they offer basics with a character and a history: jewellery from Vanrycke or the trendy Golden Goose sneakers. Some of the furniture is also for sale.

195 MOTT

Barquillo 31
Centro ⓘ
+34 913 081 280

This romantic shop merits to be called the temple of boho-chic style in Madrid. Raw linen, Japanese fabrics and silk are just some of the treasures you can find along with their collections of shoes, bags and jewellery. Most of the brands are from Spain, France and Denmark.

192 EKSEPTION

5 places for trendy
FRENCH FASHION

196 SANDRO

Claudio Coello 33
Salamanca ③
+34 914 358 521
www.sandro-paris.com

Every it-girl has something by Sandro in her wardrobe. The Paris brand from the Marais landed in Madrid in 2009 and since then has become very popular with Madrid women. Elegant and eclectic, this brand has a nice selection of statement pieces for everyday or for a special occasion.

197 MAJE

Claudio Coello 22
Salamanca ③
+34 914 359 476
www.maje.com

You might say there are some similarities with Sandro and that is because Maje was originally developed by the sister of the founder of Sandro. At Maje you will find treasures to break the dress code monotony of 9 to 5 women's workwear. Cool girls in the know will understand.

198 BA&SH

Claudio Coello 35
Salamanca ③
+34 911 383 952
www.ba-sh.com

Alexa Chung is a renowned customer of Ba&sh and Vanessa Paradis represents the Ba&sh spirit. The shop is a must go for anyone who likes a relaxed and bohemian look. Even though the brand is French, Ba&sh offers a collection that is inspired by the spirit of Ibiza.

199 THE KOOPLES

Claudio Coello 43
Salamanca ③
+34 914 355 446
www.thekooples.com

A shop for couples! Or not? The brand has been known to use anonymous and famous couples dressed in their designs for their advertising. The shop invites couples to combine their looks with a rock 'n' roll approach to fashion. The sizing runs small.

200 DES PETITS HAUTS

Claudio Coello 81
Salamanca ③
+34 914 354 203
www.despetits
hauts.com

Romantic, soft and poetic are the keywords for describing the designs of Des Petits Hauts. They are girly but not too much. Founded in 1998, they started by specialising in tops. Since then, the collection has evolved and they now sell everything, preferring to work in fabrics such as wool, cashmere and silk.

5
JEWELLERY SHOPS
for all budgets

---

201 ARISTOCRAZY
Serrano 46
Salamanca ③
+34 914 351 138
www.aristocrazy.com

Aristocrazy has taken the lead when it comes to making high quality jewellery affordable. Here you can buy pretty fashion jewellery at a very reasonable price. They are the leaders in fashion jewellery, and always on top of the latest trends. Their beautifully decorated shops could teach the big brands a thing or two.

202 APODEMIA
Goya 27
Salamanca ③
+34 918 274 795
www.apodemia.com

Inspired by nature, Apodemia's jewels are a tribute to the Apodemia butterfly that migrates from Brazil to Canada. The jewellery is romantic, feminine and made to be worn every day. Their shops hint at their source of inspiration with a splendid use of vegetation.

203 SUAREZ
Serrano 63
Salamanca ③
+34 917 819 940
www.joyeria
suarez.com

Founded in 1943 in Bilbao, Suarez opened its first Madrid shop in 1982. Since then, Suarez has been a reference for precious gems and has been known for selecting the best diamonds and pearls for their designs. The wedding rings of the current King and Queen of Spain were created by Suarez.

204 **MALABABA**

Lagasca 68
Salamanca ③
+34 912 035 990
www.malababa.com

The first Madrid store opened in 2010 but Malababa has been creating beautiful accessories and jewellery since 1997. Her style is pure and minimalist. She adds a new twist to all of her creations every season. Leather is one of her favourite materials to work with, which she uses in various forms and colours to create unique pieces.

205 **ANDRES GALLARDO**

Conde de
Romanones 5
Centro ②
+34 911 569 110
www.andresgallardo.es

This is the most avant-garde and original Spanish jeweller. Originally from Murcia he has a strong fan base of international trendsetters in the fashion and movie industry. Porcelain is broken into pieces, polished and re-assembled into subjective and surrealistic compositions.

202 APODEMIA

204 MALABABA

5 colourful
FLOWER SHOPS

206 MARGARITA SE LLAMA MI AMOR

Fernando VI 9
Centro ①
+34 913 100 926
www.margaritase
llamamiamor.com

Here they sell all kinds of flowers, some that are very difficult to find in other florists' indoor and outdoor plants, aromatics, vases and pots. They also opened the first and only store in Madrid dedicated to cacti. What makes this place unique: the space, the light, the background music and their friendliness.

207 BRUMALIS

Covarrubias 20
Chamberí ⑤
+34 912 872 090
www.brumalis.es

This is the most spectacular flower shop in Madrid. Founded by Mariluz and Loreto (whose family are antiques dealers), it is located in an old antique shop that hasn't changed in 50 years. Their inimitable flower arrangements have sealed their reputation as the wedding florist par excellence.

208 TIRSO DE MOLINA

Plaza de Tirso
de Molina
Centro ②

Tirso the Molina Square has 8 flower kiosks that are open every day of the year, which is particularly useful when you feel like buying flowers on a Sunday afternoon. What they sell may not be that eclectic, but with a little creativity you can put together a pretty flower bouquet.

209 MOSS FLORISTAS

Don Ramón
de la Cruz 51
Salamanca ③
+34 915 759 536
www.mossfloristas.com

Entering Moss is like stepping into an enchanted garden. This romantic flower shop makes some of the best flower arrangements in town. Their 'Haute Couture Flowers' arrangements, which feel rustic and uncomplicated, make them an exclusive gift or treat for your home.

210 PLANTHAE

Doctor Fourquet 30
Centro ②
+34 910 711 830
www.planthae.com

They call themselves a Botanical Cabinet. A nice and interesting shop offering a wide variety of plants as well as other products such as flowerpots and original ceramics. They also organise special events and exhibitions, which are always related to the botanical world.

206 MARGARITA SE LLAMA MI AMOR

5 lovely
BOOKSTORES
to spend hours

---

211 **PANTA RHEI**

Hernán Cortés 7
Centro ①
+34 913 198 902
www.panta-rhei.es

A bookstore dedicated to the visual arts with an emphasis on contemporary culture. Books of graphic design, advertising, the latest in exhibitions catalogues of leading artists, fashion books, special editions and illustrated children's literature. It does not end here. It is also a gallery exhibiting drawings and illustrations.

212 **LIBRERIA DESNIVEL**

Plaza Matute 6
Centro ②
+34 913 694 290
www.libreria
desnivel.com

This is the oldest bookstore in Spain still open in its original location. Specialised in mountain sports and travel: in their shelves you will find books, maps, magazines, guides, manuals and DVDs. Expert and friendly, they are always there to advise you on your search.

213 **PASAJES**

Génova 3
Chamberí ⑤
+34 913 101 245
www.pasajeslibros.com

This bookstore specialises in original works (English, French, Italian, German, Portuguese, Russian). It is one of the few bookstores where you can find a good selection of books in various languages. Named by the *Financial Times* in 2012 as one of the five best multilingual bookstores in the world.

214 CERVANTES Y COMPAÑÍA

Pez 27
Centro ⓘ
+34 910 118 037
www.cervantes
ycia.com

This small bookshop offers a selection of special editions, with second-hand books in the basement. Óscar and Maria's passion is palpable in the activities they organise, including book presentations, where you can chat with the authors, dramatised readings or concerts.

215 A PUNTO

Hortaleza 64
Centro ⓘ
+34 917 021 041
www.apunto
libreria.com

A bookstore and cooking school combined into one. At A Punto you will find the most complete selection in Madrid of books on cooking, nutrition, gastronomy and wines, with more than 5000 references. They call themselves the cultural centre of good taste.

212 LIBRERIA DESNIVEL

5 stylish
DESIGNER FURNITURE
shops

---

216 HOW
Cristo 3
Centro ⓘ
+34 917 958 420
www.how-shop.com

Hay, Norman, Hartô, Ondarreta are only a few of the contemporary and minimalist brands you will find at How. This small shop close to the Conde Duque centre offers a wide range of products that were designed and produced in Europe. They also design custom-made furniture.

217 MESTIZO
Piamonte 4
Centro ⓘ
+34 917 958 899
www.mestizostore.com

Here you will find furniture, textiles and decorative objects. With a style that holds midway between vintage and modern this 300-square metre shop is truly a treasure trove for anyone who knows how they want to decorate their home: unique, cosy, elegant and different.

218 BATAVIA
Mejía Lequerica 2
Centro ⓘ
+34 915 942 233
www.batavia.es

This is Batavia's most recent shop in Madrid, and an impressive demonstration of their ability to combine the best contemporary furniture with unique items of great beauty, from Europe and Asia. In addition to this, they also have an extensive selection of mid-century vintage furniture from northern Europe, mainly from Denmark.

219 LAGO

Velázquez 86-C
Salamanca ③
+34 915 762 077
www.lago.it

This is the Madrid shop of this prestigious Italian design furniture brand. Lago offers functional and poetic designs. With an innovative spirit and unconventional ideas, their furniture will add a touch of originality to your home.

220 BD MADRID

Villanueva 5
Salamanca ③
+34 914 350 627
www.bdmadrid-online.com

Since 1977, BD has become the reference for contemporary and modern furniture. Their showroom showcases designs by some of the leading international firms they represent such as Artek, B&B Italia, Cassina, USM Haller, Vitra, Flexform, Knoll, Fritz Hansen, BD Barcelona, Depadova, Carl Hansen, Paola Lenti, Nani Marquin and Acerbis.

217 MESTIZO

5 shops for
ESPADRILLES and
CLASSIC SHOES

221 ANTIGUA CASA CRESPO

Divino Pastor 29
Centro ①
+34 915 215 654
www.antiguacasa
crespo.com

Nowadays, the fourth generation is in charge of this unique shoe store, which opened in 1836 and is the only store in Madrid that sells espadrilles made in its own factory by its own craftsmen. Choose from hundreds of models in various styles and colours. All are handmade and a must-have for summer.

222 GLENT

Callejón Jorge
Juan 14
Salamanca ③
+34 914 315 581
www.glentshoes.com

Look no further, this is the place to go for custom-made men's footwear that is 100% made in Spain. All their models are made to order so they perfectly fit your foot, style and habits. They use a 3D scanner to measure the size, width and instep of your foot to create snug-fitting shoes. King Juan Carlos is a loyal customer.

223 CASTAÑER

Claudio Coello 51
Salamanca ③
+34 915 781 890
www.castaner.com

It all started in 1927 in Cataluña but the real success and reinvention of this espadrille maker dates from the sixties. Yves Saint Laurent happened to be at a fair in Paris and had a stroke of genius asking them to make a wedged espadrille for his fashion house. Lorenzo Castañer accepted the challenge, and that is how Castañer became the first shoe company to make this type of footwear.

224 MINT&ROSE

Santa Teresa 12
Centro ①
+34 910 719 746
www.mintandrose.com

At Mint&Rose you will find elegant espadrilles, classic high heels, Mediterranean sandals and bohemian ballerinas. The collections are inspired by summer, secrete destinations and the Mediterranean, of course. The shop became a success when the simple espadrille became a luxury shoe thanks to their unique creations and design.

225 CARTUJANO

Claudio Coello 28
Salamanca ③
+34 910 506 213
www.cartujano.com

All Cartujano products are made in Spain by expert hands after traditional methods that have been handed down for generations. Now the fourth generation of the Fluxá family is managing the brand, producing shoes with the same Goodyear sewing they introduced 139 years ago.

The 5 best
SHOPPING STREETS

226 CALLEJÓN DE JORGE JUAN
Salamanca ③

This small dead-end street starts from Jorge Juan in-between Calle Lagasca and Calle Claudio Coelio. It epitomises Madrid's true spirit, away from the big global brands that can be found in any big city. Instead this street has small boutiques of Spanish and international designers such as Anine Bing, Isabel Marrant or Angel Schlesser.

227 CALLE FUENCARRAL
Centro ①

This very popular shopping street runs from Gran Vía all the way up to Calle Sagasta. If you are looking for streetwear and sneakers, this is the perfect street for you, with all the major sport brands and smaller multi-brand stores with young designers and casual clothing.

228 CALLE CLAUDIO COELLO
Salamanca ③

This is a beautiful street with some of the best independent shops for both men and women. Nestled in the elegant Salamanca district, the street has almost no traffic (it's a one-way street) and is lined with trees on both sides. The best shops are between Calle Goya and Calle Ortega y Gasset.

227 CALLE FUENCARRAL

229 GRAN VÍA

226 CALLEJÓN DE JORGE JUAN

229 **GRAN VÍA**
Centro ①

The high-street fashion district par excellence. With flagship stores of some of the big fashion brands, Gran Vía is a favourite hangout for teenagers. At the intersection with Plaza del Callao, you walk into Calle Preciados where you will find two shops of the Spanish department store El Corte Inglés and a huge Fnac-shop.

230 **CALLE SERRANO**
Salamanca ③

Calle Serrano is the upmarket, posher version of Gran Vía. Here you will find the flagships of Luis Vuitton, Gucci or renowned Spanish fashion designers Agata Ruiz de la Prada and Roberto Verino. Even the architecture of the 5-storey Zara branch is unique. The shop is located in a refurbished building from the 1920s.

5 cool shops for
SUNGLASSES

231 ULLOA OPTICO

Serrano 21
Salamanca ③
+34 914 352 626
www.ulloaoptico.com

The Serrano shop of Ulloa was refurbished by Isabal López Vilalta in an ultra-modern, minimalist and industrial style. The history of Ulloa Optico starts in 1919 and nowadays they have 23 shops around Spain. Their sunglass brands include classics such as Ray-Ban and Persol along with the stunning designs of Chanel, Chopard or Dior.

232 ÓPTICA TOSCANA

Hortaleza 70
Centro ①
+34 913 605 007
www.opticatoscana.com

Where seeds and spices used to be sold in 1881, you can now buy shades from such sought-after brands as Illesteva, Mykita or the artistic shades of Anna-Karin Karlson. Óptica Toscana was founded in 1992 and has since become a frontrunner in fashionable eyewear.

233 L'ATELIER ÓPTICA

Moratín 18
Centro ②
+34 910 295 536
www.latelieroptica.es

Halfway between a workshop and an art gallery, L'Atelier Óptica is located in the Las Letras neighbourhood, combining Nordic style with industrial rationalism. The cosmopolitan and restless customers who are eager to stay on top of the trends come here for corrective glasses and sunglasses.

70 ROBUSTIANO DIEZ OBESO 70
ANTES 89 Y 92 · SIMIENTES, SEMILLAS · GRANOS, LEGUMBRES · ANTES 90 Y 92
CASA FUNDADA EN 1881

óptica TOSCANA

232 ÓPTICA TOSCANA

234 BLANCHE & MUTTON

Velázquez 46
Salamanca ③
+34 911 168 778
www.blanche
andmutton.com

In an immaculately white store, Blanche & Mutton are dedicated to offering the most individualised and effective optometric care for specific visual needs. They sell the coolest and most fashionable brands and have created their own designs under the name of Dr. Mutton. The Bianca model is especially elegant.

235 ÓPTICA CARIBOU

Espíritu Santo 14
Centro ①
+34 915 212 033
www.optica
caribou.com

At Caribou, you will find a selection of handmade sunglasses from niche brands catering to those who are looking for a sophisticated albeit traditional style. At Optica (accent on O) Caribou they sell international brands that are a reference in the world of sunglasses like Valley (Australia), SUPER (Italy) and Illesteva (USA).

5 specialised
RECORD STORES

236 LA INTEGRAL
León 25
Centro ②
+34 914 296 918
www.laintegral25.com

Located in a former bakery. Maria and Charo originally opened their shop to showcase their own creations. Now they offer a wide selection of brands and an extraordinary array of vinyl records, which includes reissues of great rock, pop, punk or jazz classics as well as new editions of Spanish bands of independent labels.

237 BAJO EL VOLCÁN
Ave María 42
Centro ②
+34 912 502 121
www.bajoelvolcan.es

Specialising in new and second-hand vinyl, LPs or singles of all types including soul, funk, jazz, rock 'n' roll, beat, garage, psychedelia, folk, progressive, heavy, punk and indie. Bajo el Volcán also has an interesting book section focusing on music, cinema and contemporary literature.

238 CUERVO STORE
Velarde 13
Centro ①
+34 912 222 222
www.holycuervo.com/
cuervo-store-2

Opened in 2010, Cuervo Store is a place for music, clothing, books, accessories, exhibitions and live concerts. Here you will find vinyl by Hellacopters, the Ramones or the Black Rebel Motorcyle Club. But they do even more than just merchandising. Holy Cuervo is an artist management agency and label.

239 BIG MAMMA

Divino Pastor 22
Centro ①
+34 915 915 564
www.bigmamma
cdshop.com

The store offers a wide range of new and second-hand vinyl as well as CDs. They cover all styles but have a penchant for black music including hip-hop, jazz, the blues. If you have difficulty finding what you are looking for, just ask Diego Ortiz to help you. He has overseen the inventory since 2006.

240 RADIO CITY

Conde Duque 14
Centro ①
+34 915 477 767

There is no point in describing this place. The following sample of what they offer speaks for itself: Stiff Records, Bleecker & MacDougal, Johnny Otis, Flying Nun Records, Kelley Stoltz, The Wrecking Crew, Ben Vaughn and the 1619 Broadway on 49th Street.

236 LA INTEGRAL

The 5 most interesting
VINTAGE SHOPS

241 LA MONA CHECA

Velarde 2
Centro ①
+34 915 933 997

La Mona Checa is a treasure trove for those vintage clothes and accessories that we all love so much. But you will also find a large collection of vintage cameras or the work of an unknown artist here. As they like to say about themselves, they are halfway between a grandmother's house and a circus.

242 IKB 191

Arganzuela 18
Centro ②
+34 918 259 591
www.ikb191.es

Located in the Rastro area, in a former garage, this huge shop is now home to a neo-antiquarian who believes that vintage furniture shouldn't break the bank. Here you will only find original European furniture from the forties and fifties, and not necessarily from famous designers. Vintage, affordable design for everyone.

243 MAGPIE

Velarde 3
Centro ①
+34 914 483 104
magpie.es

Specialising in vintage clothing and accessories from the twenties, sixties and seventies, this shop has the most glorious array of hats, headgear, belts, handbags and footwear in Madrid. Past lucky finds included a Valentino bathing suit, and even a Balenciaga dress.

244 MODERNARIO

Santa María 20
Centro ②
+34 913 697 678
www.modernario.es

With two shops on the same street, Modernario is your first stop in Madrid for vintage furniture and lighting from the fifties, sixties and seventies. Only well-known designers and brands including Hans Wegner, Finn Juhl, Arne Jacobsen, Verner Panton, Charles and Ray Eames, Frank O. Gehry, Louis Kalff and Le Corbusier.

245 FLAMINGOS VINTAGE KILO

Espíritu Santo 1
Centro ①
+34 915 048 313
www.vintagekilo.com

Here you can buy vintage and second-hand clothing by the kilo, with prices ranging from just 7 to 18 euros a kilo. Think classic Levis 501s, Hawaiian shirts, bomber jackets, sports shorts for men, Navajo style women's clothing, military fatigues, seventies dresses, leather, tuxedos and cowboy boots.

242 IKB 191

EDIFICIO METROPOLIS

25 BUILDINGS TO ADMIRE

5 buildings in the MADRID
OF THE AUSTRIAS —————————————— 134

5 secrets about PLAZA MAYOR ——————————— 136

5 striking examples of MODERN
and CONTEMPORARY architecture—————————— 138

5 impressive and elegant GATES ——————————— 141

5 must-see ICONIC buildings ———————————— 143

5 buildings in the
MADRID OF
THE AUSTRIAS

**246 COLEGIATA
E INSTITUTO
DE SAN ISIDRO**
Toledo 37
Centro ②

Mary of Austria, daughter of Charles V, bequeathed her fortune to the Jesuits, allowing them to build this jewel of the Madrilenian Baroque. The building has a stunning inner patio and is famous for being the Alma Mater of the most outstanding writers in Spanish literature.

**247 MINISTERIO
DE ASUNTOS
EXTERIORES**
Juan de Mena 4
Retiro ④

Today this building is home to the Spanish Ministry of Foreign Affairs but it used to be the Court Jailhouse. On 2 May 1808, its doors where unlocked allowing the prisoners to help defend the city of Madrid. Legend has it that each and every one of the prisoners returned to their cells of their own volition after the French were defeated.

**248 ANTIGUO MUSEO
DEL EJÉRCITO/
SALÓN DE REINOS**
Méndez Núñez 4
Retiro ④

This building, which will be incorporated in the Prado in 2019, and the Cason del Buen Retiro, are all that remains of a large architectural complex that was commissioned by Felipe IV as a second residence and which also marked the eastern limits of the city of Madrid in 1630.

249 PALACIO DE LOS DUQUES DE UCEDA

Mayor 79
Centro ②

Built in the 17th century, the Palace of the Dukes of Uceda has always accommodated the most powerful and important councils of the Spanish monarchies since the 16th century: from the Councils of Castile and Indias to the most recent Spanish State Council and the General Captaincy.

250 MONASTERIO DEL CORPUS CHRISTI

Plaza del Conde de Miranda 3
Centro ②

Known as the Convent of the Carboneras. The nuns and the convent took their name from a painting of the virgin that was found in a nearby coal yard and donated to the nuns. The hidden courtyard patio and the homemade cakes the nuns sell are the best kept secrets of this place, which has remained virtually untouched since it was built 400 years ago.

248 ANTIGUO MUSEO DEL EJÉRCITO/ SALÓN DE REINOS

5 secrets about
PLAZA MAYOR

251 LAMPPOSTS
Centro ②

Engraved in four lampposts are images that tell the history Plaza Mayor. From 1609 until 1822, trials were held here, there was a huge fire in 1790, a farmers market, a bullfighting arena in the 1620s and a square where lavish masked gatherings were held in the 17th and 18th century.

252 BULLFIGHTS
Centro ②

In 1619, Plaza Mayor hosted bullfights to commemorate important festivities. There were two bullfights every day: a morning session for the common people and an afternoon bullfight for the King and Nobles at double the price. The last bullfight took place in 1846 to celebrate the double wedding of Isabel II and her sister María Luisa.

253 HELL ALLEY
Centro ②

This gloomy alley was given the rather majestic name of Victory Arch Street in 1854, but is more popularly known as Hell Alley (Callejón del Infierno) after huge flames came out at the other end in Calle Mayor, during the second, most brutal fire in Plaza Mayor in 1672.

254 THE PULPIT INSIDE THE CUTLERS ARCH
Centro ②

Inside the Cutlers Arch (Arco de Cuchilleros) there is a discrete stone platform with a semi-circular metallic handrail that played a surprisingly decisive role in the history of Madrid. It was here that the monk Antonio rallied a large crowd of Madrilenians against the French invader in 1808, starting the War of Independence.

255 LAGOON
Centro ②

At the end of the 16th century, Plaza Mayor did not exist yet. The muddy lagoon of Lujan, which used to be here, was a popular duck hunting spot for kings and also served as a primitive farmers market on the outskirts of the village of Madrid. Felipe II designated Madrid as capital of the kingdom, transforming the lagoon into a square inspired by the Roman Forum.

251-255 **PLAZA MAYOR**

5 striking examples of
M O D E R N and
C O N T E M P O R A R Y
architecture

256 **BBVA LAS TABLAS**

Sierra de
Atapuerca 31
Las Tablas

Inspired by ancient Roman cities, 2001 Pritzker laureates Herzog & de Meuron designed this office complex of seven horizontal 3-storey buildings which cover a massive surface area of 114.000 square metres, which are connected with patios and gardens. An innovative 93-metre-tall and 13-metre-wide sail-shaped main building, where 6000 employees work, rises up in the main square.

257 **JERONIMOS EXTENSION OF THE PRADO MUSEUM**

Paseo del Prado s/n
Retiro ④

Designed by Rafael Moneo, the first extension of the Prado Museum outside the Villanueva building was erected on the demolished remains of the cloister of the Church of St. Jerome. A large subterranean hall was excavated to connect the Villanueva building with the new building, and a large brick cube which has the same shape as the cloister and which is considered controversial sits atop the hall.

258 CEPSA TOWER

Paseo de la
Castellana 259-A
Tetuán ⑥

Standing at 248 metres tall, this is the second tallest building in Spain and the fourth tallest in Europe. It was designed by Sir Norman Foster around two massive steel and concrete pillars that accommodate seven elevators. Between them, a 'shelving unit' was created with three intermediate platforms, bearing the weight of up to twelve storeys each.

259 BARAJAS TERMINAL 4

Barajas

Inaugurated in 2006 and designed by Richard Rogers in collaboration with the Spanish Studio Lamela, these two buildings make up the newest terminal of Madrid's airport named 'T4'. The metallic undulating roof, which is covered on the interior with bamboo, is supported by columns that have been placed at an angle and are colour coded.

260 TORRES DE COLÓN

Plaza de Colón
Centro ①

These 23-storey twin skyscrapers were built in 1976 and designed by the Spanish architect Antonio Lamela. Built from top to bottom around two massive pillars that are joined at the top by a platform, the Art Deco 'plug' was added in the nineties to hide the antennas and technical facilities on the rooftop. It gave rise to its nickname, the plug.

257 JERONIMOS EXTENSION OF THE PRADO MUSEUM

264 PUERTA DE ALCALÁ

262 PUERTA DE FELIPE IV

5 impressive and elegant
GATES

261 PUERTA REAL

Paseo del Prado,
Jardín Botanico
Retiro ④

This is what is left of Francesco Sabatini's – the favourite architect of Charles III – original design for the Royal Botanical Gardens in 1773. Juan de Villanueva modified it to such an extent that this former main entrance gate was shut ever since in favour of the gate that faces the Prado Museum.

262 PUERTA DE FELIPE IV

Alfonso XII s/n,
Retiro Park
Retiro ④

Built in 1680, this is the oldest of all the monumental gates in Madrid. Designed by the architect Melchor de Bueras, it commemorated the arrival of Queen Marie-Louise of Orleans, the first wife of Charles II. It also served as a gateway to the set of buildings and gardens that constituted the Palacio del Buen Retiro.

263 PUERTA DE HIERRO

Gta. Puerta
de Hierro s/n
Moncloa-Aravaca

Named after its characteristic closed iron gate below the arch. This gate was built during the reign of Fernando VI in 1751 and was located on the outskirts of the city, serving as the main gateway to the king's private hunting grounds.

264 PUERTA DE ALCALÁ

Plaza de la
Independencia
Salamanca ③

This is one of the monumental icons of the city of Madrid. It was constructed by Francesco Sabatini in 1778 to commemorate the arrival of king Charles III in Madrid and was installed on the road to Alcalá de Henares from which it takes its name. Made of granite with a neoclassical style, this is a perfect example of architectural proportion and harmony.

265 PUERTA DE TOLEDO

Glorieta Puerta de
Toledo s/n
Centro ②

Construction started during Joseph Bonaparte's reign, but after the French were defeated, Fernando VII chose to build a gate instead in order to commemorate his arrival in the city of Madrid. The sculptures above the central arch, which overlook both sides, represent the power of the Spanish monarchy in both hemispheres of the world.

5 must-see
I C O N I C *buildings*

266 **EDIFICIO METRÓPOLIS**
Alcalá 42
Centro ②

With 30.000 24ct gold leaves covering parts of its marvellous dome, this is one of the most beautiful buildings in Madrid, especially when it lights up at night with its 205 lights. Inaugurated in 1911, seven houses were demolished in this privileged location to make way for its construction. The insurance company Metropolis, which gave its name to the building, bought it in 1972.

267 **EDIFICIO ESPAÑA**
Plaza de España
Centro ①

A project of the Otamendi brothers inspired by the Rockefeller Plaza, this building was inaugurated in 1953 as a propaganda icon of the prosperous Spain of General Franco. Thirty-two elevators were used to transport celebrities and Franco's high society entourage to its 25 floors with 300 offices, 184 apartments, an exclusive hotel, a shopping mall and an Olympic pool on the rooftop.

268 ESTACIÓN DE ATOCHA

270 PALACIO DE CIBELES

269 PALACIO DE CRISTAL

268 ESTACIÓN DE ATOCHA

Plaza Emperador
Carlos V
Arganzuela ⑧

Inaugurated in 1892, this building was initially called Estación de Mediodia (Station). In 1992, it was renovated by Pritzker Laureate Rafael Moneo and turned into a railway station with a metro station, a mid and short distance train station, high speed trains and a fantastic large tropical garden inside the original station's gigantic iron structure.

269 PALACIO DE CRISTAL

Paseo República
de Cuba 4
Retiro ④

Built for the Universal Exposition of the Philippines in 1887, this building was designed by Ricardo Velázquez Bosco and inspired by London's Crystal Palace in Hyde Park. It moved to Retiro Park after the Exposition. Surrounded by buckeye trees and with an artificial lake in front of it, the building is sometimes used as a modern art exhibition space for the Reina Sofía museum.

270 PALACIO DE CIBELES

Plaza Cibeles 1
Centro ②

This project by Joaquin Otamendi and his university friend Antonio Palacios was inaugurated in 1909 as the headquarters of the National Post and Telegraph company. Nowadays it is home to Madrid's town hall, a post office, a vibrant cultural centre and a rooftop restaurant and bar with one of the best panoramic views of the city.

PARQUE DE EL CAPRICHO

55 PLACES
TO DISCOVER
MADRID

5 **PARKS** *that are as nice as El Retiro* —————— 148

5 *secret spots inside* **EL RETIRO** —————— 150

5 **SQUARES** *to discover* —————— 152

5 *walks through 5* **NEIGHBOURHOODS** ——— 154

5 *things to do during the* **SAN ISIDRO** *festival* — 156

5 '**LA MOVIDA**' *hangouts* —————— 158

5 *must-visit sites for* **REAL MADRID** *fans* ——— 160

5 *secret and stunning* **PALACES** —————— 162

5 **STATUES** *inspired by intriguing legends* ——— 164

The 5 best **STREET ART** *scenes* ——————— 166

5 *interiors by* **UP-AND-COMING**
DESIGNERS —————————— 168

5 PARKS

that are as nice as El Retiro

---

271 PARQUE JUAN CARLOS I

Glorieta Sar Don
Juan de Borbon y
Battermberg s/n
Barajas

Juan Carlos I is an immense 160-hectare park with 2000 olive trees. The park was inaugurated the same year that Madrid was the European capital of Culture (1992) and is home to a wonderful sculpture collection. The lake and estuary are used for water sports such as canoeing or fishing. A small train runs through the park every 30 minutes.

272 PARQUE DEL OESTE

Paseo de Moret 2
Moncloa-Aravaca ②

This 100-hectare park, close to Plaza de España, is the work of famous landscape designer Cecilio Rodriquez and was built under the governance of Alberto Aguilera in 1906. It hosts many attractions such as the Madrid cable car, a rose garden with a yearly contest and the Temple of Debod, a gift from the Egyptian Government.

273 PARQUE QUINTA DE LOS MOLINOS

Alcalá 527
San Blas

At the very end of Calle Alcalá, you will run into this 28-hectare garden. Its origin goes back to 1920 when the owner of the estate chose to create a Mediterranean garden. In the northern part, you can enjoy a romantic landscape while the southern part of the garden is more agricultural in character. The park is planted with 8000 trees. The almond trees flower in February and March.

274 PARQUE DE EL CAPRICHO

Paseo de la Alameda de Osuna 25
Barajas

Next to Juan Carlos I park you will find one of the most beautiful parks and, paradoxically, the most unknown park in Madrid. Created in 1784 by the Dukes of Osuna, it has three different styles: French parterre, English landscape and aspects of an Italian giardino with plenty of romantic fountains and temples.

275 REAL JARDÍN BOTÁNICO

Plaza de Murillo 2
Retiro ④

The park is a good representation of the local vegetation in combination with a tropical garden. Its original landscape was designed by Francisco Sabatini, who received the commission from Fernando VI in 1755. Admission to the garden is 4 euros. All funds are used to maintain the park and its 5000 species of plants, flowers and trees.

5 secret spots inside
EL RETIRO

---

276 PEACOCKS

Jardines de Cecilio
Rodríguez
Paseo Uruguay 5
Retiro ④

In the Gardens of Cecilio Rodriguez there are small ponds, water springs, sculptures, climbing vines with columns and pergolas, benches in the shade, trimmed hedges, hidden corners and peacocks. You will spot the peacocks around the main fountains or hear them in the trees.

277 LA ROSALEDA

Paseo Fernán Núñez 4
Retiro ④

The Rose Garden reveals its full splendour during the months of May and June, when roses bloom. Designed by Cecilio Rodríguez in 1915, the garden is planted with just under 4000 roses. It is said that there once used to be a pond here, which was as an ice-skating rink in winter, when it froze.

278 ORCHARD

Avenida de
Alfonso XII s/n
Retiro ④

Here the aim is to develop an environmental education programme focusing on ecological agriculture and gardening and to promote more environmentally responsible behaviour among the population. Various activities, presentations and guided tours are organised for both adults and children.

279 BIBLIOTECAS POPULARES

Paseo Fernán
Núñez 24
Retiro ④

In 1919, small free-standing libraries were built in the Parque del Retiro, with different books and some related to nearby monuments to promote reading. In 1994, the Madrid Book Fair decided to rehabilitate two of these structures to promote bookcrossing between anonymous readers.

280 TENNIS, PADDLE AND SOCCER

Paseo Fernán
Núñez 3
Retiro ④

In the heart of the park, hidden behind trees, there is a sports centre with tennis and paddle courts and a football pitch. The centre is managed by the town council and the prices are very affordable. You can rent a tennis court for 7,50 euros. They offer plenty of classes and activities for children.

279 BIBLIOTECAS POPULARES

5

SQUARES

to discover

---

281 PLAZA DE LA PAJA
Centro ①

Nestled in the Madrid of the Austrias, this small square makes you feel as if you are in a village. Its name refers to past activities as the straw for the mules of Capilla del Obispo was auctioned here. Have a beer on one of the terraces and dinner or lunch at the Naia restaurant.

282 HUERTO DE LAS MONJAS
Sacramento 7
Centro ②

At number 7 on Sacramento Street you will find the small entrance to the Huerto de las Monjas. After you have walked through a passage under modern buildings, the charming garden reveals itself to you. Until 1972, it was protected by the high walls of a convent (that was demolished).

283 JARDINES DEL PALACIO DEL PRÍNCIPE DE ANGLONA
Príncipe Anglona 1
Centro ②

At the bottom end of Plaza de La Paja, there is a very small and romantic garden. The original 1750 structure was maintained when it was created for the adjacent noble house where the Prince of Anglona used to live. A pleasant hideaway and a good place for a break from the hectic city centre.

284 PLAZA DEL ÁNGEL

Centro ②

This quiet square is located next to the very busy and crowded Plaza Santa Ana with its taverns and tapa restaurants. The elegant Palace of Tepa (now a NH hotel) overlooks the square, which is also home to Café Central, which opened in 1910. Nowadays Central is a meeting point for live music lovers.

285 PLAZA DE LA VILLA DE PARÍS

Centro ①

Hidden behind the Colon Centre, this beautiful square is also called the square of Justice. Tucked in between the Supreme Court, the National High Court and L'Institut Français (The French Institute) it has an open space with trees and benches. It is also the meeting place for the neighbourhood dogs and their owners.

283 JARDINES DEL PALACIO DEL PRÍNCIPE DE ANGLONA

5 *walks through*
5 NEIGHBOURHOODS

286 CHAMBERÍ
Chamberí ⑤

If you are into cuisine, then head to Calle Ponzano or to Olavide Square in Trafalgar with its cosy garden and terraces for some tapas. The district became really glamorous in the 19th century, when Madrid's aristocracy moved here. Zurbano Street is still one of the most prestigious addresses in Europe (according to the *New York Times*).

287 BARRIO DE LAS LETRAS
Centro ②

This bohemian and artistic neighbourhood with its narrow streets almost makes you feel as if you are in a Castilian village. Take a walk down Calle del León, Calle del Prado, Calle Cervantes and Calle Lope de Vega. Literary figures of the Spanish Golden Age such as Lope de Vega, Quevedo, Góngora and Cervantes used to live here.

288 LAS SALESAS

Centro ①

Named after the church, this neighbourhood is considered to be the Soho of Madrid. The main streets to discover are Calle Almirante, Calle Barquillo and Calle Fernando VI. Don't be afraid to walk in the adjacent small streets, as there are plenty of cool shops, galleries and bars to discover.

289 SALAMANCA

Salamanca ③

Madrid's chicest and most glamorous neighbourhood, with the main shopping streets running parallel to each other: Calle Serrano, Calle Claudio Coello and Calle Lagasca. The statue of its founder is in Marques de Salamanca Square which intersects with the high-end Calle Ortega y Gasset.

290 LAVAPIÉS

Centro ②

This neighbourhood is a melting pot of people and cultures. The abundance of Indian restaurants in Calle Lavapiés is just one sign of this. In Calle Argumosa there is a bustling bar and tapas scene that has been taken over by young entrepreneurs because the rents are lower here. A bit further down in Plaza de Lavapiés you will run into Tabacalera, a massive street art centre.

5 things to do during the
SAN ISIDRO *festival*

---

291 PRADERA DE SAN ISIDRO

San Isidro Park,
Paseo de la Ermita
del Santo 74
Carabanchel

On the morning of May 15th, at the San Isidro park, everybody enjoys typical Madrid dishes from the food stands while listening to Chulapo music. The Parade of the Giants and Cabezudos (big heads) winds its way through the park and traditional Zarzuelas and comic operas are performed.

292 FIREWORKS

Retiro Park
Retiro ④

The fireworks displays around the pond in Retiro are an amazing experience. They are organised on Saturday and Sunday night during San Isidro weekend and are a great family outing. Remember, the park closes its doors at midnight.

293 COCIDO MADRILEÑO

Bola 5
Centro ②
+34 915 476 930
www.labola.es

The best place to enjoy a traditional Cocido Madrileño is at La Bola. Start with a vegetable soup, made with the broth of the stew, after which you eat the cooked meat and sausages with chickpeas. Since 1870, La Bola has been serving this traditional dish, which is still made according to the original recipe. Book in advance.

294 LAS VENTAS

Alcalá 237
Salamanca ③
www.las-ventas.com

Recognised as the most important bullring in the world, Las Ventas comes to life every year on the occasion of San Isidro. From May until the end of June, some of the best Spanish and international bullfighters fight corridas here. There are also two chapels here, one of which is dedicated to la Paloma, one of Madrid's patron saints.

295 SOUND ISIDRO

www.soundisidro.es

During the whole month of May, Sound Isidro organises concerts in various concert venues across the city such as El Sol, Barceló Theater, Moby Dick or Riviera. Up to 50 bands participate in the festival. Innovation and musical quality are the criteria for selecting the artists.

294 LAS VENTAS

5

'LA MOVIDA'

hangouts

---

296 EL SOL

Jardines 3
Centro ②
+34 915 326 490
www.salaelsol.com

This concert hall was founded by Antonio Gastón, an architect who was passionate about music and art. The first ever concert here was by Nacha Pop in 1979. Since then, it has been part of the Movida and its glamour. Hundreds of major Spanish and international pop rock artists have stood on stage here.

297 LA VÍA LÁCTEA

Velarde 18
Centro ①
+34 914 467 581

It all began in July 1979. As the Movida movement gathered steam, the square of Dos de Mayo and the surrounding area were always bustling with young and curious people who attended any cultural and fun event. The bar's founder wanted to copy the aesthetics and ambiance of the New York musical bars.

298 EL PENTA BAR

Palma 4
Centro ①
+34 914 478 460
www.elpenta.com

This iconic bar in the Madrilenian Movida was originally called the Pentagram but the name was soon shortened to Penta. Forty years ago, the musicians of the eighties helped spread the movement out of this bar, where a lot of Spanish pop music was developed.

299 MADRID ME MATA

Corredera Alta
de San Pablo 31
Centro ①
+34 609 847 504
*www.madrid
mematabar.com*

The bar was named after a popular eighties magazine that was more or less the mouthpiece for the Nueva Ola (New Wave), which over time became known as the Movida. Nowadays the bar is almost like a museum, with many items on display such as books, clothing, records and instruments.

300 LA BOBIA

San Millán 3
Centro ②
+34 917 376 030

The only Movida bar where the interior and theme have changed. Nowadays it is a cosmopolitan neo-tavern serving Asturian food. Here filmmakers like Fernando Fernán Gómez and Pedro Almodóvar filmed their movies. The terrace is still there, albeit with newer models of the mythical light green chairs.

300 LA BOBIA

5 must-visit sites for
REAL MADRID *fans*

---

301 ESTADIO SANTIAGO BERNABÉU

Avenida de Concha Espina 1
Chamartín ⑦
www.realmadrid.com

The home stadium of Real Madrid. Also a museum. Take a tour of the stadium, which includes a visit to the trophy room, a panoramic view of the pitch, the presidential box and the locker rooms. The stadium also has four restaurants and the Real café, all offering great views.

302 CIUDAD REAL MADRID

Camino Sintra s/n
Valdebebas
www.realmadrid.com

These are the training facilities where the players train every day and also the home of the future elite of the club. Every day you can see journalists and fans at the entrance gate, jostling to get a good picture or an autograph of the players as they arrive and leave.

303 SANCHIS BAR MARISQUERÍA

Avenida de Menéndez Pelayo 13
Retiro ④
+34 915 742 429

Not every Madrid player becomes a coach after hanging up his cleats. Manolo Sanchis, who played as a sweeper and appeared in more than 700 official games from 1983 to 2001, took over his father's bar. His father also was a Real Madrid player. A must-see for true Real Madrid fans.

304 **MESÓN TXISTU**

Plaza Ángel
Carbajo 6
Tetuán ⑥
+34 915 701 006
www.mesontxistu.com

It is not unusual to see the president of Real Madrid having lunch with players of his team at Mesón Txistu. This elegant Basque restaurant serves traditional cuisine from the north. Cristiano Ronaldo has been spotted here many times, enjoying a nice meal.

305 **EL TULIPÁN**

General Díaz
Porlier 59
Salamanca ③
+34 914 025 027

This small bar has more than 2500 football jerseys, both from Atletico and Real Madrid. Most players signed theirs and each team has its own space in the restaurant to avoid conflicts. The bar serves simple, homemade food, from Asturias.

301 **ESTADIO SANTIAGO BERNABÉU**

5 *secret and stunning*
PALACES

―――――――――

306 PALACIO LONGORIA

Fernando VI 4
Centro ①

The palace stands among the surrounding 19th-century buildings and surprises nearby pedestrians. Built in 1902, it has a luxurious and ornate façade, in the typical Art Nouveau style. Some mistakenly think it was designed by Gaudi. Nowadays it is the headquarters of the Society of Spanish writers and editors.

307 WUNDERHOUSE

San Lorenzo 20
Centro ①
+34 915 990 369
www.wunder-
house.com

The palace is now the most stunning student halls of residence in the world. The setting is stunning as it used to be the residence of the Marques Villa Magna in 1870, after which it was owned by the Vatican until 1994. The palace has original frescos and has been completely refurbished.

308 FUNDACIÓN CARLOS DE AMBERES

Claudio Coello 99
Salamanca ③
+34 914 352 201
www.fcamberes.org

Since 1594, the foundation has assisted travellers coming to Madrid from the 17 provinces of the Netherlands. As of 1988, it is dedicated to maintaining the cultural and historic relationships with the Netherlands, Belgium, Luxembourg and northern France.

309 PALACIO DE FERNÁN NÚÑEZ

Santa Isabel 44
Centro ②
+34 911 511 082
www.ffe.es/palacio

While this neo-Classical palace may look simple from the outside, its secrets are hidden within. It was built in 1753 and since 1985 it has been the headquarters of the Foundation of the Spanish Railways. Inside all the elements of the wealthy 19th-century aristocracy have been preserved. Group visits only. They must be booked in advance by calling the Foundation.

310 PALACIO DE LIRIA

Princesa 20
Centro ①
+34 915 481 550
www.fundacioncasa
dealba.com

Nestled in lush gardens, this 18th-century palace was once the home of the flamboyant Duquesa de Alba. Only the façade was left standing after the Civil War. Following the Duquesa's death in 2014, at the ripe old age of 88, you can now discover the home and art collection of the Dukes of Alba on Fridays.

307 WUNDERHOUSE

5

STATUES

inspired by intriguing legends

---

311 THE FALLEN ANGEL
Glorieta del Ángel Caído s/n, Retiro Park
Retiro ④

The statue represents Lucifer as he is expelled from heaven. Legend has it that this is a gateway to hell. Why? Because the statue stands at 666 metres above sea level. This may also have something to do with the disappearance of the old cemetery after the construction of the Paseo Fernán Nuñez.

312 JULIA
Pez 42
Centro ①

She is not very tall and is leaning very discreetly against the wall of Calle del Pez 42. Her legend started more than 150 years ago, when only men were allowed to study at the university. Julia dressed up as a man and made it onto the San Bernardo central university benches. The statue honours her since 2003.

313 THE BEAR AND THE STRAWBERRY TREE
Plaza Puerta del Sol
Centro ②

The symbols go back to medieval times when Madrid's coat of arms was designed. The bear was chosen as an emblem in honour of a brown bear that King Alfonso XI hunted. Initially he was represented with a tower until disputes over land with La Villa were resolved and Madrid was given grazing land, with strawberry trees.

314 PLAZA DE ORIENTE
Centro ②

The 108 statues of medieval Spanish kings originally were to be installed on the cornices of the Royal Palace. A dream or perhaps a premonition of Queen Bárbara de Braganza led to a change of plans. She saw them falling down during an earthquake and convinced her son to move them somewhere safer.

315 FELIPE III
Plaza Mayor
Centro ②

When the Second Republic was proclaimed in 1931, some vandals put a firecracker in the slightly open mouth of the horse. The stomach of the horse exploded. People started to say that the horse would come back to life at night to hunt with the spirit of the king. But the truth was that curious birds entering through the mouth of the horse became entrapped in it.

314 PLAZA DE ORIENTE

The 5 best
STREET ART
scenes

---

316 YIPI YIPI YEAH

Argumosa 25
Centro ②
www.yipiyipiyeah.com

A Madrid street art community whose work is always surprising and full of irony and humour. They share their political views and aspects of pop culture along with the absurdity of our world. Head to their favourite neighbourhoods of Malasaña and Lavapiés, La Latina and the Barrio de las Letras.

317 HYURO

Embajadores 68
Centro ②
www.hyuro.es

With her art, this Argentinian urban artist shows how women carry the weight of the patriarchal society. Her creative universe is full of women. They are caregivers, housewives and mothers, all lacking an identity. Seductive and mysterious, her militant works pop in urban areas.

318 BOA MISTURA

AT: MERCADO DE LA CEBADA
Plaza de la Cebada
Centro ②
www.boamistura.com

This multidisciplinary team of five artists are developing their graffiti art in Madrid as well as in South Africa, the USA, the UK and Brazil. Besides the roof of Cebada Market you will also find their art works in many other parts of Madrid like in the Barrio de las Letras.

319 ELTONO

Espoz y Mina 9
Centro ②
www.eltono.com

Eltono is from France and has been working in Madrid for the past decade, after which he moved to Beijing and now he lives in the south of France. His work is inspired by the public space where his sensitivity is expressed in art combined with the unpredictable character and whims of the street.

320 MUROS TABACALERA

Embajadores 51
Centro ②
www.muros
tabacalera.com

This project could be the beginning of a Madrid Wynwood. Muros is a project that covers the walls of the outer perimeter of the courtyard of the Tabacalera, turning them into urban art spaces for the enjoyment of everyone. In its first year, in May 2014, 32 artists created 27 interventions. Since then every year the art walls are refreshed, with new artists or new works.

320 MUROS TABACALERA

5 interiors by
UP-AND-COMING
DESIGNERS

---

321 ONE SHOT HOTEL
BY LAS 2 MERCEDES
Salustiano Olózaga 4
Salamanca ③
+34 911 820 070
www.hoteloneshot
recoletos04.com
www.las2mercedes.com

The One Shot is a cool and extremely well-located 4-star hotel dedicated to art and photography. The two friends, who are originally from Seville, decorated the 60 rooms and the public spaces. They had started out decorating private homes and then came the One Shot project providing a canvas for their eclectic style, in which they mix classic pieces with other more modern designs.

322 LA FÁBRICA DE CAMISAS
BY LOUIS GARCÍA FRAILE
Paseo de la Habana 33
Chamartín ⑦
+34 917 047 588
www.lafabrica
decamisas.com
www.lgfstudio.com

Luis García Fraile mainly designs private homes but when he is asked to design commercial projects, he interprets spaces in an elegant and witty way with a clever mix of fabrics, materials and styles.
His interiors are Spanish, infused with influences from his international travels and experiences.

323 EL IMPARCIAL

BY MADRID IN LOVE

Duque de Alba 4

Centro ②

+34 917 958 986

www.elimparcial
madrid.com

www.madrid
inlove.com

This über-cool restaurant close to Tirso de Molina is located in what used to be the headquarters of the Imparcial newspaper. Today it is a café, restaurant, shop and cultural space. An all in one space decorated by the interior design collective of Madrid in Love. They combine innovation and tradition and are experts when it comes to giving something old a new lease on life.

324 NAVAJA

BY TATIANA GARCÍA BUESO

Valverde 42

Centro ①

+34 636 852 304

www.restaurante
navaja.com

www.espacios
dearquitectura.com

Navaja is dedicated to razor clams and ingredients from Galicia mixed with Japanese influences. The interior resonates perfectly with the menu thanks to the work of Tatiana. She infused the space with a minimalist shabby chic style and recycled materials. More of her work can be seen at Juanita Banana and at the Malayerba barber shop.

325 BENARES

BY COUSI INTERIORISMO

Zurbano 5

Chamberí ⑤

+34 913 198 716

www.benares
madrid.com

www.cousiinteriorismo
yeventos.es

The London-based Indian chef chose Madrid after his Mayfair success, working with Cousi Interiorismo to provide a wonderful backdrop for his excellent cuisine. Alicia and Alba, whose project name is inspired by the English word cosy, created an elegant restaurant with a classic and sophisticated style.

MUSEO NACIONAL CENTRO DE ARTE REINA SOFÍA

50 PLACES TO ENJOY CULTURE

5 secrets about 5 **MUSEUMS** —————— 172

5 of the most interesting **FOUNDATIONS** ———— 174

5 amazing **ART GALLERIES** —————— 176

5 artsy **STREETS** and **CENTRES** —————— 178

5 places for **LIVE MUSIC** —————— 180

5 tablaos with the best **FLAMENCO SHOWS** —— 182

5 **CHURCHES AND CATHEDRALS**
to admire —————————— 184

5 of the many **THEATRES** to visit —————— 186

5 **CINEMAS** with films in the original version —— 188

5 recurring cultural **EVENTS** not to miss ———— 190

5 secrets about 5
MUSEUMS

326 PRADO MUSEUM

Paseo del Prado s/n
Retiro ④
+34 902 107 077
www.museodelprado.es

By the end of the 19th century, the Prado was almost abandoned and bonfires were lit inside by the workers. Mariano de Cavia became so desperate about the state of the building that he published a fake news item titled 'Fire at the Prado Museum!!'. People were so moved that the government had no choice but to take action.

327 MUSEO DEL ROMANTICISMO

San Mateo 13
Centro ①
+34 914 481 045
museoromanticismo.
mcu.es

A reinterpretation of a 19th-century tearoom, the courtyard patio has the perfect combination of jazz and music to chill out to at the right sound level, creating an inviting atmosphere to read or have a chat over delicious pastries. With plants, trees and a central fountain, it's the ideal place to escape from Madrid's summer heat.

328 MUSEO NACIONAL CENTRO DE ARTE REINA SOFÍA

Santa Isabel 52
Centro ②
+34 917 741 000
www.museoreina
sofia.es

A fantastic option for breakfast or a coffee. The terrace in the beautiful garden of the 18th-century Sabatini building is surrounded by majestic trees, fountains and sculptures from the museum's collection. It is the perfect place to start or end your visit to the museum.

329 ABC MUSEO DE DIBUJO E ILUSTRACIÓN

Amaniel 29-31
Centro ①
+34 917 588 379
museo.abc.es

This modern museum was built in 2014 on the remains of the very first Mahou brewery, the most popular and oldest beer brand of Madrid. The new building is a fascinating architectural exercise by studio Aranguren & Gallegos. A 4-storey cube with two subterranean floors where geometry and natural light are combined to create a magnificent space.

330 MUSEO SOROLLA

Paseo del General
Martínez Campos 37
Chamberí ⑤
+34 913 101 584
www.mecd.gob.es/
msorolla

Sorolla was one of the most sought out paintors of his time, especially in American high society. In 1909, Louis Comfort Tiffany, the son of the famous jeweller, bought various paintings and commissioned a portrait from him. The admiration was mutual, Sorolla bought three lamps from the Tiffany Glass Company that are still on display in his museum house today.

5 of the most interesting
FOUNDATIONS

---

331 FUNDACIÓN JUAN MARCH

Castelló 77
Salamanca ③
+34 914 354 240
www.march.es

Not many locals know that they are welcome to discover unique exhibitions of 20th-century artists for free in this space. The exhibits change every 3 months and offer an interesting mix of works by contemporary artists and lesser-known figures from key artistic movements. The small shop has amazing posters that you won't usually find in the traditional museum shops.

332 ESPACIO FUNDACIÓN TELEFÓNICA

Fuencarral 3
Centro ①
+34 915 808 700
www.fundacion
telefonica.com

Located inside Telefonica's historic headquarters in the heart of Gran Vía, this building was inaugurated in 1929 and became Spain's very first skyscraper. For 25 years, it was the tallest building in the city. Nowadays it is an alternative art space, as well as host to a permanent exhibition on the history of telecommunications.

333 FUNDACIÓN MAPFRE

Paseo de Recoletos 23/
Bárbara de Braganza
13
Centro ①
+34 916 025 221
+34 915 816 100
+34 915 814 609
*www.fundacion
mapfre.org/fundacion*

The foundation has two locations.
The first one is an old palace in Paseo
Recoletos, which every season hosts
some of the hottest international
painting and sculpture exhibits in town.
The second location is in Calle Bárbara
de Braganza and only hosts photo
exhibitions, with the work of talented
young artists and acclaimed artists
being shown in one space.

334 CAIXAFORUM

Paseo del Prado 36
Centro ②
+34 913 307 300
*agenda.obrasocial.
lacaixa.es*

The iconic building by Herzog & de
Meuron is in itself a piece of art. The
former electric power plant has been
transformed into a floating cube with
a unique vertical garden. Visitors enter
the building and ascend a striking
spiral staircase that takes them to the
exhibition galleries, which always host
fresh, new art exhibitions.

335 FUNDACIÓN FRANCISCO GINER DE LOS RÍOS

Paseo del General
Martínez Campos 14
Chamberí ⑤
+34 914 460 197
*www.fundacion
giner.org*

Home of the Free Teaching Institution,
a movement supported by members
of academia in the thirties. Two of the
original pavilions have been renovated
and now connect, in an architectural
game of volumes, to this new 5000 sq.m.
building that is clad with galvanised steel
bars and has an amazing auditorium
inside.

5 amazing
ART GALLERIES

336 MONDO GALERIA

San Lucas 9
Centro ①
+34 913 082 325
www.mondo
galeria.com

Specialising in photography and design, this gallery has a photo library with an impressive collection of works. Every week they organise seminars, workshops and masterclasses by the artist they promote. A way to get closer to their work and better understand their artistic approach.

337 GUILLERMO DE OSMA

Claudio Coello 4
Salamanca ③
+34 914 355 936
www.guillermo
deosma.com

Since their opening in 1991, this gallery has hosted more than 80 exhibitions dedicated to modern and contemporary art, taking a special interest in the historic European and Latin-American vanguards (1910-1939). Every year, they take part in the major contemporary art fairs.

338 HELGA DE ALVEAR

Doctor Fourquet 12
Centro ②
+34 914 680 506
www.helga
dealvear.com

Established in Madrid since 1995, this is currently one of the most widely respected galleries on the Spanish art scene with an international reputation: more than 900 square metres dedicated to international contemporary art.

339 MOISÉS PÉREZ DE ALBÉNIZ

Doctor Fourquet 20
Centro ②
+34 912 193 283
www.galeriampa.com

This is one of the coolest art spaces in Madrid, which has been in business for over 20 years. Its exterior wall is constantly renovated and used to exhibit works, as part of the gallery. They promote young talent and like to combine it with more renowned international artists.

340 IVORYPRESS

Comandante Zorita 46-48
Tetuán ⑥
+34 914 490 961
www.ivorypress.com

Founded in 1996 by Elena Ochoa Foster as a publising house, this is the best art library in Madrid, covering a wide range of areas and activities within the framework of contemporary art. On Wednesdays, you can take a free guided tour of its permanent art collection, with works by Michael Long, Duchamp or Damien Hirst.

339 MOISÉS PÉREZ DE ALBÉNIZ

5 artsy
STREETS *and* CENTRES

341 BARRIO DE LAS LETRAS

Centro ②
www.barrioletras.com

Where writers such as Cervantes, Lopez de Vega or Gongora once used to live, a vibrant cultural scene is now emerging in the backyard of Madrid's triangle of art museums. Here you have new wave artisan shops, art galleries, fabulous interior design shops, a unique short film festival (Notodofilmfest) and the National Photo festival (Photoespaña).

342 MATADERO MADRID

Plaza de Legapzi 8
Arganzuela ⑧
+34 915 177 309
www.matadero
madrid.org

What used to be Madrid's slaughterhouse along the Manzanares river in 2013 was turned into one of the most comprehensive cultural centres in the city. Its seven different spaces accommodate any kind of artistic expression, including music concerts, film, photography and painting exhibits.

343 LA CASA ENCENDIDA

Ronda de Valencia 2
Arganzuela ⑧
+34 902 430 322
www.lacasa
encendida.es

This centenary building is now a cultural centre that supports innovation and cutting-edge artwork. It has an amazing, dynamic programme that includes exhibits, lectures and cinema series, as well as conferences, debates and one of the best art libraries in Madrid.

344 CALLE DEL DOCTOR FOURQUET

Centro ②

For the last 20 years, art galleries have been concentrated in this small street just behind the Reina Sofía. Considered the most important art street in Spain, its 15 galleries coordinate their exhibits, always welcoming visitors that are interested in checking out emerging and more established modern artists.

345 CENTRO CULTURAL CONDE DUQUE

Conde Duque 11
Centro ①
+34 913 184 450
www.condeduque
madrid.es

These former military barracks were transformed into one of the most important cultural spaces dedicated to creativity in Madrid in the seventies. Home to the archive of the city of Madrid and one of the biggest public libraries, it is a popular venue for modern music concerts, dance festivals, temporary art exhibits and a summer cinema in its open patio.

345 CENTRO CULTURAL CONDE DUQUE

5 places for
LIVE MUSIC

---

346 COSTELLO CAFE & NITE CLUB

**Caballero de
Gracia 10**
Centro ②
+34 915 221 815
www.costelloclub.com

The space has three different ambiences: The Golden Lounge on the ground floor which is a great bar for drinks. Walk through a narrow hallway to get to a chill out space with white beds named the White Lounge. The best of Madrid's undergound bands perform live every week on the stage of the basement Club area.

347 LA RIVIERA

**Paseo Bajo de la
Virgen del Puerto s/n**
Centro ②
+34 913 652 415
www.salariviera.com

With two or three shows a week, its capacity for over 2500 people and a unique curved shape that makes for perfect acoustics and viewing, this has become one of the most important venues for live music in Madrid, hosting international bands and world-class DJs for more than 50 years now.

348 EL JUNCO

**Plaza de Santa
Bárbara 10**
Centro ①
www.eljunco.com

This is a refuge for night owls and a sanctuary for live music fans. Every day of the week, El Junco pays tribute to the best of black music. They offer everything, from jazz to funk through soul, hip hop and even Brazilian fusion, and jam sessions (Tuesday to Thursday nights).

349 MOBY DICK

Avenida de Brasil 5
Tetuán ⑥
+34 915 557 671
www.mobydick
club.com

Opened in 1992 and dedicated to national and international emerging independent band, this is a popular place with fans of live music. The interior is clad in wood and is shaped like an inverted ship, providing perfect acoustic quality. Thanks to its small size, every concert becomes special. A fun bar, with no cover, after the show has ended.

350 SALA CLAMORES

Alburquerque 14
Chamberí ⑤
+34 914 455 480
www.salaclamores.es

This small venue has been one of the temples of live music in Madrid since its opening in 1983. It started out as one of the few jazz clubs and evolved, initially offering some blues, fado and funky music and then a wider range of live shows including some of the best Cuban musicians, flamenco singers and tribute bands.

5 tablaos with the best
FLAMENCO SHOWS

---

351 CORRAL DE LA MORERÍA

Morería 17
Centro ②
+34 913 651 137
*www.corral
delamoreria.com*

Founded in 1956 and once frequented by Frank Sinatra and Ava Gardner, this was named the best flamenco tablao in the world by the prestigious Festival del Cante de las Minas. Blanca del Rey, National Flamenco Award and the widow of its founder Manuel del Rey, personally selects the artists that will perform that night.

352 CASA PATAS

Cañizares 10
Centro ②
+34 913 690 496
www.casapatas.com

A charming tavern, specialising in tapas and Spanish gastronomy, which has become a major flamenco venue in the capital. Many figures in the modern flamenco world, from Estrella Morente to Tomatito or Pepe Habichuela, have delighted the audience with their art and talent.

353 CAFÉ DE CHINITAS

Torija 7
Centro ②
+34 915 471 502
www.chinitas.com

Located on the groundfloor of a 17th-century palace, this place takes its name from a famous café in Malaga, which was frequented by Picasso and Dali and cited in a poem by Lorca. Its iconic stage, surrounded by colourful manila shawls, every night welcomes some of the best flamenco performers.

354 VILLA-ROSA

Plaza de Santa Ana 15
Centro ②
+34 915 213 689
www.tablaoflamenco
villarosa.com

During the twenties, this place became a legendary *tablao*, thanks to the distinguished flamenco singer Don Antonio Chacón, where noblemen and even the king himself could secretely enjoy private flamenco parties in its downstairs VIP rooms.

355 TORRES BERMEJAS

Mesonero
Romanos 11
Centro ②
+34 915 310 353
torresbermejas.com

Opened in 1960, with an interior decoration that reproduces the Torres Bermejas of the Alhambra, this is where the best flamenco singer and legend Camarón was presented to Madrid. He sang here for twelve years and here is also where he met the virtuous guitarist Paco de Lucía.

5 CHURCHES and CATHEDRALS
to admire

---

356 BASÍLICA SAN MIGUEL
San Justo 4
Centro ②
+34 915 484 011
www.bsmiguel.es

It was built in 1739 with a rather noticeable Italianate influence. Despite its small size, this is one of the most relevant buildings in the city of Madrid, because of its singular interpretation of the Spanish Baroque, thanks to its unique convex façade.

357 CHURCH OF SAN MANUEL Y SAN BENITO
Alcalá 83
Salamanca ③
+34 914 357 682
www.samasabe.es

Built in 1910, this church became the headquarters of the Executive Committee of the Communist Party during the war (1936). Its dome is one of the best examples of neo-Byzantine architecture in Madrid. The inner side of the dome is profusely decorated with mosaics representing 16 saints of the order of Saint Augustine.

358 CHURCH OF SANTA BÁRBARA

General Castaños 2
Centro ①
+34 913 194 811
www.parroquiade
santabarbara.es

In 1757, Queen Bárbara de Braganza decided to create a palace to retire, a monastery and a feminine institution that was similar to the Seminar, that educated young noble boys destined to occupy top positions in society. In 1870, General Prim transformed the entire complex except the church into law courts, where the Spanish Supreme Court has its seat today.

359 CHURCH OF SAN ANTONIO DE LOS ALEMANES

Puebla 22
Centro ①
+34 915 223 774

Built in 1624, near the Portuguese hospital, the church and the hospital were named after San Antonio de los Alemanes soon after Portuguese independence. With its discrete façade, the elliptic interior is why visiting this place is so important. Its walls are covered with impressive frescos representing the life of Saint Anthony of Padua.

360 CHURCH OF SAN ANDRÉS APÓSTOL

Plaza San Andrés 1
Centro ②
+34 913 654 871
www.iglesia
sanandres.es

With its distinctive tower and dome, this is one of the oldest churches in Madrid. It was built on the remains of a 12th-century church where Saint Isidro, the patron saint of Madrid, used to pray. The current building dates from the 17th century and was completely restored in 1986 after an intentional fire in 1936.

5 of the many
THEATRES
to visit

---

361 MICROTEATRO POR DINERO

Loreto Prado y Enrique Chicote 9
Centro ①
+34 915 218 874
www.microteatro.es

A new theatre concept, with a bar and 15-minute microplays, on a specific theme, which are performed in six different spaces for an audience of 15 people tops. This makes the theatre more accessible and more affordable, giving new authors and playwrights a break.

362 TEATRO DE LA ZARZUELA

Jovellanos 4
Centro ②
+34 915 245 400
teatrodelazarzuela. mcu.es

Commissioned by the Spanish Opera Society and inaugurated on Isabel II's birthday in 1856, this theatre was used for the performance of zarzuela. In 1984, the Spanish government took over the building. Now it also hosts performances by dance and flamenco companies.

363 TEATRO CALDERÓN

Atocha 18
Centro ②
+34 914 294 085
teatrocalderon.es

Probably one of the most beautiful buildings in Madrid because of its majestic exterior and interiors. It was inaugurated in 1917. Originally built for opera performances, the theatre can accommodate an audience of more than 1000 people. Nowadays international shows are staged here.

364 TEATRO LARA

**Corredera Baja
de San Pablo 15
Centro ①
+34 915 239 027
*www.teatrolara.com***

The theatre was commissioned in 1879 by Candido Lara, a self-made man who paid his way up in society. No expense was spared for this theatre, which was inspired by the Parisian Palais Royal. The very best and most expensive Spanish productions were performed on this stage and it is still very popular with theatre-goers today.

365 TEATRO LUCHANA

**Luchana 38
Chamberí ⑤
+34 910 075 684
*www.teatrosluchana.es***

The old Luchana made way for a new theatre, with several halls, that caters to all kinds of audiences. The programme changes continuously, with productions by young theatrical companies. This is the theater to go to if you like alternative theater and love to have many options to choose from.

362 TEATRO DE LA ZARZUELA

5

CINEMAS

with films in the original version

---

366 YELMO IDEAL

Doctor Cortezo 6
Centro ②
+34 913 691 053
yelmocines.es/
cartelera/madrid/
yelmo-cines-ideal

Built in 1916, this place became very popular with horror film fans, as so many triple bills were screened here. The colourful windows on the first floor still refer to the building's original use, with several mysterious figures. Inside, in nine theaters, you can see the latest blockbusters and alternative international films.

367 CINES RENOIR RETIRO

Narváez 42
Retiro ④
+34 915 422 702
www.cinesrenoir.com

This cinema belongs to one of the biggest cinema chains in Madrid. It only shows films in their original version with subtitles. There are five different theatres that screen the latest international alternative cinema hits.

368 PEQUEÑO CINE ESTUDIO

Magallanes 1
Chamberí ⑤
+34 914 472 920
www.pcineestudio.es

José Gago is the man behind this personal tribute to the very best of the classic cinema since its opening in 1973. This tiny, cosy place (only 124 seats) is an institution for classic cinema fans and one of the few places to enjoy fantastic films by Pasolini, Truffaut, Fassbinder or Fellini on the big screen.

369 CINE DORÉ

Santa Isabel 3
Centro ②
+34 913 693 225
www.mecd.gob.es/
cultura-mecd/areas-
cultura/cine/

This elegant Art Nouveau building is home to the Spanish National Film Library. Founded more than 50 years ago, it is a must-see for any film buff. Film series with films by acclaimed international directors of all eras at affordable prices. (Tickets are just 2,5 euros). Buy your tickets in advance.

370 CINE ESTUDIO

AT: CÍRCULO DE BELLAS
ARTES
Marqués de Casa
Riera 4
Centro ②
+34 915 213 509
www.circulobellas
artes.com

Since its reopening in 1999, with its own original programme, this place has continued to be one of the cult spots for film fans. Its film series regularly pay tribute to acclaimed actors and directors that are now part of the history of cinema. Each ticket comes with a leaflet explaining every aspect of the film.

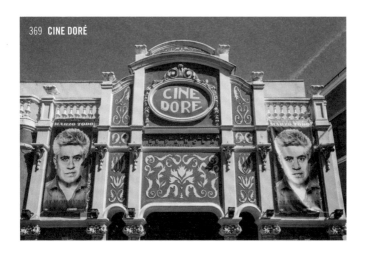

369 CINE DORÉ

5 recurring cultural
E V E N T S *not to miss*

---

371 CASA DECOR
+34 917 556 834
www.casadecor.es

Once a year for 40 days, new and renowned interior designers, architects and furniture brands get together to completely refurbish every room of an abandoned or soon-to-be-demolished building, in what is considered a unique oportunity in Europe to see the latest trends in interior design.

372 PHOTO ESPAÑA
+34 913 601 326
www.phe.es

This international photo festival started in 1998 and has grown over the years becoming a reference in the visual arts. Its exhibits can be found in the city's museums, galleries and even in stores, making this the biggest and most popular event that takes place every summer in Madrid.

373 ARCOMADRID
AT: FERIA DE MADRID
**Avenida del
Partenón 5
Barajas
+34 902 221 515**
*www.ifema.es/
arcomadrid_01*

ARCO is the acronym for the International Contemporary Art Fair. Celebrated every February in Madrid since 1982, it has become one of the leading international art fairs. From the historic vanguards to the emerging artists of today, ARCO acts as a stimulus for the Spanish art scene.

374 MULAFEST

AT: FERIA DE MADRID
**Avenida del
Partenón 5
Barajas
+34 902 221 515**
www.mulafest.com

Every summer, this young urban festival provides a platform for new ways of expression and living. Artists can show off their graffitti, tattoo, malabarism, skating, music or clothing design skills. You can even have a bike customised here. Visitors can check out the fair on their skatebords or chill on the artificial beach.

375 VERANOS DE LA VILLA

*www.veranosde
lavilla.com*

Madrid would not be the same in July and August without its amazing array of concerts, shows, activities and open air cinema festivals. Promoted by the city council and the main leisure centres of the capital, its absolute highlights are the summer night concerts in the Jardines de Sabatini.

MUSEO NACIONAL DE CIENCIAS NATURALES

25 THINGS TO DO WITH CHILDREN

5 fun OUTDOOR ACTIVITIES —————————— 194

5 RESTAURANTS to go with kids ————————— 196

The 5 coolest TOY SHOPS ——————————— 198

5 MUSEUMS kids will love——————————— 200

The 5 cutest CHILDREN'S
CLOTHING SHOPS ———————————— 202

5 fun
OUTDOOR ACTIVITIES

376 **ZOO AQUARIUM OF MADRID**

Casa de Campo s/n
Moncloa-Aravaca
+34 902 345 014
www.zoomadrid.com

The 20-hectare zoo and aquarium in Casa de Campo Park is home to more than 6000 animals. It was founded in 1770 and today has one of the most impressive collections of marine wildlife in Europe. Get there by Metro line 10.

377 **FAUNIA**

Avenida de las
Comunidades 28
Vicálvaro
+34 902 535 545
www.faunia.es

Reproducing various ecosystems and their plants and animals, Faunia is a fun educational activity. It takes four to five hours to walk through the park and discover the various ecosystems that have been recreated here such as the jungle, the African forest or the Polar circle. Open from March to the end of September.

378 **WARNER PARK**

A-4 highway, exit 22
San Martín de la
Vega
www.parque warner.com

The park has five areas and immerses you in the Warner Bross Universe with its Hollywood Boulevard, Movie World Studios, Old West Territory, Cartoon Village and Super Heroes World. You'll feel like you are walking through movie sets. Check their website for more information on how to get there, by bus or train.

379 MADRID FLY

Avenida Ntra. Señora
del Retamar 16
Las Rozas de Madrid
+34 912 648 353
madridfly.com

This is the largest wind tunnel in Europe: 4,6 metres wide and 17 metres high. The project was launched a few years ago by a parachuting champion. His aim was to simulate free flying in absolute safety. Children must be at least 5 years old.

380 SPORT HIELO

Silvano 77
Hortaleza
+34 917 160 159
www.sporthielo.com

Right next door to the Palacio de Hielo shopping centre and cinemas, the ice-skating facilities are a great place to learn and practise ice-skating. You can rent skates on site. Do not forget to bring gloves. Sport Hielo is open from September to June.

5
RESTAURANTS
to go with kids

---

381 KILÓMETROS DE PIZZA

Zurbano 26
Chamberí ⑤
+34 910 612 474
www.kilometros
depizza.com

Here pizza is served by the metre and the largest is 2 metres long. You can choose various toppings for each half metre. The pizzas are huge, look fun, and also taste good, which is a plus. They are homemade with Italian flour and cooked in the largest pizza oven in the world, which was custom-built for the restaurant by Castelli.

382 LA CABAÑA MARCONI

Camino del Cura 233
Encinar de los Reyes
+34 916 507 913
www.cabana
marconi.com

A 10-minute taxi ride from the centre and you will find yourself at the Cabaña Marconi. Parents will love the sun-drenched dining rooms with a Scandi feel. Meanwhile, the kids can play and make new friends in the surrounding garden. The owner's Swedish-Mexican background is reflected in the menu.

383 LOS KIOSCOS OF THE FLORIDA RETIRO

Paseo República
de Panamá 1
Retiro ④
+34 918 275 275
www.floridaretiro.com

In the heart of Retiro Park, the newly opened Florida Retiro offers a beautiful outdoor terrace with plenty of interesting food options. Eat on the premises or put together a take-out picnic for in the park. Each of the seven kiosks offers a different theme, from seafood to tapas.

384 FILANDON

Carretera
Fuencarral-El Pardo
(M-162), km 1,9
El Pardo
+34 917 343 826
www.filandon.es

On the way to El Pardo, you will run into Filandón. This enormous farmhouse, which has been renovated and modernized, stands on a 9000 sq.m. parcel of land. The perfect place for a long lunch, while your children explore the huge garden.

385 COSTELLO RÍO

Plaza General
Maroto 4
Arganzuela ⑧
+34 914 737 205
www.costellorio.com

Inspired by American diners, Costello Río is a great option after a stroll through Madrid Río. The menu is a child's dream come true: a hamburger with a milkshake. With its bright, big interior and cool music, Costello is a fun place for the whole family. They use recycled elements such as pallets for the tables and cans for the lamps.

383 LOS KIOSCOS OF THE FLORIDA RETIRO

The 5 coolest
TOY SHOPS

---

386 IMAGINARIUM
Carmen 15
Centro ②
+34 915 238 729
www.imaginarium.es

This Spanish toy brand was created in 1992 and now has more than 400 stores around the world. They owe their success to the rigorous selection of toys for babies and children up to 75 years old. The shop is always easy to recognise because of the special kids' entrance.

387 DON JUEGO Y DON PUZZLE
Alcalá 113
Salamanca ③
+34 914 314 349
www.donjuego.es

Don't be fooled by its size, this is the shop which has almost every puzzle and board game known to man. Here you can find all kinds of games: strategy, family, solitary, classic, theme, skills and for children. They also have a stock of 1700 different puzzles.

388 TIENDAS ASÍ
Principe de Vergara 12
Salamanca ③
+34 915 751 367
www.tiendas-asi.com

A family business that was founded in 1942. The shops are called the houses of dolls and sell an original selection of dolls, plush toys, accessories, doll houses and their furniture, costumes, collector's dolls, porcelain dolls and rag dolls. In 1965, they began to create and produce their own doll models.

389 MACCHININE

Barquillo 7
Centro ①
+34 917 010 518

A shop that kids and adults will love and a real paradise for car lovers. Macchinine sells miniature cars, from different periods (antiques, originals and replicas), in various sizes and types (static, ancient and modern). They have more than 10.000 cars in stock.

390 BABY DELI

Alcalá 91
Salamanca ③
+34 915 763 810
www.babydeli.com

Baby Deli is a store, a cafeteria with an area for the kids to play and they offer fun workshops from Monday to Saturday. In the shop, they sell food, personal hygiene products, cosmetics, ecological cotton clothing, stationery, books, videos, music, gifts and toys.

390 BABY DELI

389 MACCHININE

5

MUSEUMS

kids will love

---

391 MUSEO DE CERA

Paseo de Recoletos 41
Salamanca ③
+34 913 194 681
*www.museocera
madrid.com*

The Madrid wax museum first opened its doors in 1972. Since then, it has added hundreds of identical copies of famous movie stars, football players, politicians and historical figures to its collection. Travel through time in forty rooms, with a sound and light show for each wax figure.

392 MUSEO DEL TRAJE

Juan de Herrera 2
Moncloa-Aravaca ②
+34 915 504 700
museodeltraje.mcu.es

The Costume Museum opened its doors in 2004 and has an interesting collection of original costumes from the 16th and 17th centuries. Some of the most impressive exhibits include skirts and underskirts and some excellent examples of men's attire, like 18th-century jackets.

393 MUSEO DEL FERROCARRIL

Paseo de las
Delicias 61
Arganzuela ⑧
+34 902 228 822
*www.museodel
ferrocarril.org*

Located in an old 19th-century train station, the museum was inaugurated in 1984. Discover a complete collection of historical locomotives and railway carriages in mint condition. Children learn while having fun through all kinds of activities and workshops related to the railroad.

394 MUSEO NACIONAL DE CIENCIAS NATURALES

José Gutiérrez Abascal 2
Chamartín ⑤⑦
+34 914 111 328
mncn.csic.es

A museum dedicated to fossils, meteorites, minerals, rocks and the human evolution in which you can take a journey through the history of our Earth, with a tour of fossils of all geological ages. The skeletons of dinosaurs and large mammals are the protagonists of the exhibit.

395 THE ROBOT MUSEUM

Alberto Aguilera 1
Centro ①
+34 914 478 808
www.therobot museum.eu

A small but curious museum that can only be visited with a guide, who will explain the peculiarities of each robot and demonstrate their capabilities. They have Honda's famous Asimo robot, R2-D2 from *Star Wars,* as well as the largest collection of robots in Europe.

394 MUSEO NACIONAL DE CIENCIAS NATURALES

The 5 cutest
CHILDREN'S
CLOTHING SHOPS

396 BONNET À POMPON

Lagasca 88
Salamanca ③
+34 910 609 915
bonnetapompon.com

The most impressive children's shop in Madrid with interiors designed by Lázaro Rosa-Violán. Their collections cater to children from 0 to 12 years old and mix a bohemian chic style with simple designs and more traditional pieces. This brand is a firm favourite with many mothers because of its sweet and sophisticated colours.

397 NICOLI

Lagasca 61
Salamanca ③
+34 914 472 202
www.nicoli.es

The shop for all kids from 0 to 18 years old. Elegant and relaxed collections that are pleasing to look at. And in addition to their clothing line, they have all kinds of accessories: shoes, bags, scarves, necklaces, bracelets, headgear and a million other things. A place to dress your kids from head to toe.

398 BILLIESMARKET

Hermosilla 29
Salamanca ③
+34 912 694 124
www.billiesmarket.fr

All the clothes have something different, a fun twist, something out of the ordinary with dinosaurs, sequins, superheroes or tutus. You will be hard pressed to find these original designs anywhere else. They also sell gifts including dolls, moustaches or hairbands.

399 NANOS

Hermosilla 21
Salamanca ③
+34 915 764 447
www.nanos.es

Spain is known to dress their children with very good taste and to impress. With more than 50 years of experience, Nano caters to boys and girls, babies and juniors. The complete wardrobe is available: coats, jerseys, dresses, pants, shorts, shirts, hoods, caps and scarves, leggings and communion dresses.

400 SUEÑOS POLARES

Regueros 10
Centro ①
+34 913 086 675
*www.suenos
polares.com*

Sueños Polares is a multi-brand shop selling clothing and accessories for children from 0 to 16 years old. Organic fabrics, wool and quality are their hallmark along with a creative collection of accessories. Here you can mix and match until you find the perfect outfit for your child.

396 BONNET À POMPON

30 PLACES
TO SLEEP

The 5 best **BOUTIQUE HOTELS** —————— 206

5 splendid **LUXURY HOTELS** ——————— 208

5 hotels with a **SWIMMING POOL** ————— 210

5 of the best **DESIGNER HOSTELS**
and **BUDGET HOTELS** ———————— 212

5 hotels with a **HISTORY** ————————— 214

5 cool **TOURIST APARTMENTS** ————— 216

The 5 best
BOUTIQUE HOTELS

401 HOTEL ÚNICO

Claudio Coello 67
Salamanca ③
+34 917 810 173
www.
unicohotelmadrid.com

With 44 modern rooms and the marvellous restaurant of Ramón Freixa (2 Michelin stars), the 5-star Hotel Único is the jewel in the crown of Calle Claudio Coello. The 19th-century building has been refurbished to perfection, with a modern lobby with two cosy living rooms. The hidden garden is the perfect place for a refreshing escape after a long day of shopping.

402 ONLY YOU BOUTIQUE HOTEL MADRID

Barquillo 21
Centro ①
+34 910 052 746
www.onlyyou
hotels.com

This hotel really is a work of art. It is located in a 19th-century building and each of the spaces has a distinctive personality thanks to the work of Lázaro Rosa Violán: the reception with its wall of white suitcases or the striking covered patio where the lobby is located or the homey feel of the 125 rooms. The 4-star hotel's bar and restaurant attract a hip local crowd.

403 DEAR HOTEL

Gran Vía 80
Centro ①
+34 914 123 200
www.dearhotel
madrid.com

Located on the corner of Plaza de España, Dear Hotel is a quiet oasis above the hectic Gran Vía. Just a five-minute walk from several restaurants, shops and theatres, this 4-star hotel has a Scandi feel to it, resembling a cosy and elegant temporary home. All rooms boast a street view. Check out their impressive rooftop terrace.

404 HOTEL 7 ISLAS

Valverde 14
Centro ①
+34 915 234 688
www.hotelsiete
islas.com

Located in a quiet street adjacent to Gran Vía, the main attraction at Hotel 7 Islas is the interior design. Furniture by Borge Mogensen and Ilmari Tapiovaara combines beautifully with the rustic industrial style of Kikekeller design studio. The three suites have a private terrace with great downtown views.

405 HOTEL TÓTEM

Hermosilla 23
Salamanca ③
+34 914 260 035
www.totem-
madrid.com

Located in the heart of Salamanca, Tótem is the latest snazzy 4-star addition to the Madrid Boutique hotels scene. With sleek interiors and an open space lobby, with a cocktail bar the locals flock to for drinks. Each of the 63 rooms is decorated in its own style, with specific fabrics and a personality but all have an elegant black marble bathroom.

5 splendid
LUXURY HOTELS

406 GRAN MÉLIA PALACIO DE LOS DUQUES

Cuesta de Santo
Domingo 5–7
Centro ②
+34 915 416 700
www.melia.com/gran-
melia-palacio-de-los-
duques

Located in what used to be the important Convent of Santo Domingo in the 13th century, the hotel emerges as the most impressive luxury hotel in the Madrid of the Austrias. 1000 square metres of contemporary design, 180 rooms whose interiors are inspired by the legendary *Las Meninas* painting of Velázques.

407 THE PRINCIPAL MADRID HOTEL

Marqués de
Valdeiglesias 1
Centro ①
+34 915 218 743
www.theprincipalma-
dridhotel.com

Right next to the mythical Metropolis, The Principal has a unique location, in a stunning Renaissance building. The interior is a mix of styles, from a classic British mansion to a French palace, and the 76 rooms have a decidedly masculine downtown Manhattan loft style.

408 HOTEL URSO

Mejía Lequerica 8
Centro ①
+34 914 444 458
www.hotelurso.com

The first 5-star hotel in the Tribunal and Barceló market area, with 78 rooms, a restaurant and a great spa. Cosy and modern interiors in shades of green, grey and beige come together in a chic and discreet interior design.

409 AC SANTO MAURO

Zurbano 36
Chamberí ⑤
+34 913 196 900
autograph-hotels.
marriott.com

Situated in the very elegant and exclusive Almagro residential area, the Palace of the Duke of Santo Mauro was built in the late 1800s and was converted into a luxury hotel many years ago. The hotel's neo-classical French-inspired interior still makes you feel as if you are visiting the Duke for the weekend.

410 VILLA MAGNA

Paseo de la
Castellana 22
Salamanca ③
+34 915 871 234
www.villamagna.es

A member of the Leading Hotels of the World. Villa Magna is located right next to the main shopping and leisure points of interest in the city. Don't be fooled by the dank concrete building. Once you enter, the classic style blends in perfectly with the contemporary facilities. The hotel is very popular with businessmen visiting the city.

407 THE PRINCIPAL MADRID HOTEL

5 hotels with a
SWIMMING POOL

411 HOTEL EMPERADOR

Gran Vía 53
Centro ①
+34 915 472 800
www.emperador
hotel.com

The impressive building of Hotel Emperador (232 rooms) sits right in the middle of Gran Vía. It is a classic hotel with classic rooms. However, head to the roof of the hotel and you will discover the biggest and most impressive swimming pool in the city. The pool is also open to the public if you buy a daily pass of 48 euros.

412 ROOM MATE ÓSCAR

Plaza Pedro
Zerolo 12
Centro ①
+34 917 011 173
room-matehotels.com

Óscar, the gay-friendly hotel of the successful Spanish Room Mate hotel group, is located in Pedro Zerolo Square. Its 79 original and colourful rooms are always fully booked when Chueca hosts events. The swimming pool and bar are on the rooftop terrace. It is a popular hangout for an aperitivo on summer nights.

413 HOTEL WELLINGTON

Velazquez 8
Salamanca ③
+34 915 754 400
www.hotel-
wellington.com

The Wellington, on Velazquez and very close to Retiro Park, is the Grande Dame of Madrid. The 5-star hotel opened its doors in 1952 and since then plenty of royals, movie stars and politicians have walked through them. The superb swimming pool, located on the roof of the first floor in the inner court, has a nice bar.

414 HOTEL URBAN

San Jerónimo 34
Centro ②
+34 917 877 770
www.hotelurban.com

A member of Design Hotels, Urban has a steel and glass facade that conceals a few secrets. First, the hotel has an astounding art collection with unique pieces such as a 2000-year-old Buddhist figurine. Second, the rooftop terrace has a small but comfortable swimming pool with stunning views of the city.

415 NH COLLECTION COLÓN

Marqués
de Zurgena 4
Salamanca ③
+34 915 760 800
www.nh-hotels.com

This upscale NH hotel is particularly well located, overlooking Castellana and Colón Square. It was completely refurbished in 2016. The 146 rooms have a modern and sleek design mixing white and light greys. The solarium and swimming pool on the fourth floor are spacious and very comfortable.

412 ROOM MATE ÓSCAR

5 of the best
DESIGNER HOSTELS
and BUDGET HOTELS

416 UHOSTEL
Sagasta 22
Chamberí ⑤
+34 914 450 300
www.uhostels.com

Located in a 19th-century building that has been completely renovated, Uhostel proves you can enjoy perks at a very affordable price. This hostel offers the same quality and service as a hotel and at the same time you still enjoy a traditional hostel experience.

417 PRAKTIK METROPOL
Montera 47
Centro ②
+34 915 212 935
www.praktik
metropol.com

Praktik Metropol is located in the city centre at the top of the revamped Calle Montera. The rooms are pristine and white, with vintage furniture and a Scandinavian touch. The magic happens on the ninth floor, however, where a stunning terrace offers a panoramic 360° view and loungers.

418 THE HAT
Imperial 9
Centro ②
+34 917 728 572
thehatmadrid.com

Set in a refurbished 19th-century building between Sol and La Latina. The Hat, with 42 functional rooms, has plenty of surprises in store for you. In the retro-chic lobby you can sample the foods at the gastro bar. The main attraction is the rooftop terrace with an open-air barbecue, temporary exhibits and DJ sessions.

419 SLEEPN ATOCHA

Doctor Drumen 4
Centro ②
+34 915 399 807
www.sleepnatocha.com

SleepN Atocha is one of the latest budget hotel projects in Madrid. It has a super cool and neat design. When you enter and see the lobby it is difficult to believe that room rates start from 41 euros per night. What's more, it is located just a five-minute walk from the best museums: Reina Sofia, Prado and Thyssen.

420 ROOM 007

Hortaleza 74
Centro ①
+34 913 688 111
www.room007.com

This urban hostel in Calle Hortaleza, which is just 100 metres from Chueca Square, offers value for money. 32 rooms in an industrial style, including doubles, triples or multiples (4 to 11 beds). All the rooms have their own bathroom. A cool restaurant to have lunch and dinner, an attic lounge to watch movies and yes, a small rooftop terrace.

417 PRAKTIK METROPOL

5 hotels with a
HISTORY

421 RITZ MADRID (MANDARIN ORIENTAL)

Plaza de la Lealtad 5
Retiro ④
+34 917 016 767
www.mandarin
oriental.com

Inaugurated by King Alfonso XIII in 1910. The King was the first to be aware of how much the city would gain if it had a large luxury hotel. At the time, having four or five bathrooms on each floor and a telephone next to the elevator was considered the epitome of luxury.

422 NH CASA SUECIA

Marqués de Casa
Riera 4
Centro ②
+34 912 000 570
www.nh-hoteles.es

Inaugurated as the house of Sweden in 1956 by the Swedish Royal family, it is now known as Casa Suecia. It has always been a meeting point for Swedish companies and personalities such as Harald Elling Nordin. In the late fifties and sixties, it was the home of Ernest Hemingway and Che Guevara's hotel during his one-off Madrid visit.

423 THE WESTIN PALACE

Plaza de las Cortes 7
Centro ②
+34 913 608 000
www.westinpalace
madrid.com

The Westin Palace was built on the site that was vacated after the demolition of the Palace of the Dukes of Medinaceli, a modest testimony to what had originally been the Duke of Lerma's Palace. It was so large that it resembled a city rather than a residence. Costing 15 million pesetas (90.000 euros), it was completed in 18 months and became the largest hotel in Europe in 1910.

424 ME MADRID REINA VICTORIA

Plaza de
Santa Ana 14
Centro ②
+34 912 764 747
www.melia.com

Designed and built by the Spanish architect Jesus Carrasco-Muñoz y Encina from 1919 to 1923, it only became a hotel in 1986. Prior to this, it was a department store called the Almacenes Simeón. At one point, it was also popularly known as the 'Hotel of the Bullfighters' as bullfighters during the San Isidro festivities liked to get dressed in the hotel.

425 AC PALACIO DEL RETIRO

Alfonso XII 14
Retiro ④
+34 915 237 460
www.marriott.com

This palace was built after the design of José Luís Oriol Urigüen, in 1913 and 1914, as a residence for his extended family. In 2002, it was renovated and transformed into a modern hotel, by one of his heirs, Miguel de Oriol and Ibarra. Currently it has been rented to the Hotel AC Palacio del Retiro, which was inaugurated in 2004.

5 cool
TOURIST APARTMENTS

426 ERIC VÖKEL

San Bernardo 61
Centro ①
+34 934 334 631
www.ericvokel.com

Located just a few steps from Calle de la Palma and Plaza 5 de Mayo, the whole building has cool apartments with a neat design and a hint of Barcelona in the mosaic tiles. They are fully equipped and have a reception service. The penthouse apartments have a splendid private terrace.

427 GRAN VÍA CAPITAL

Gran Vía 48
Centro ①
+34 910 284 776
www.granviacapital.es

This building by the Spanish architect Rafael de la Hoz is the first to be built along Gran Vía since 1932. Here we have the ultimate in luxury apartments. Some of the services and amenities include: a jacuzzi on the 13th floor, sauna, gym, parking, 24 hours/7 days a week front desk service.

428 ASPASIO BOUTIQUE APARTMENTS

San Mateo 16
Centro ①
+34 618 767 147
www.aspasios.com

These apartments are nicely located in the Justicia neighbourhood. Each apartment is elegant and comfortable combining modern elements with the original details of the building. The 2-bedroom terrace apartment is really nice and starts from 100 euros per night.

429 **60 BALCONIES RECOLETOS**

Almirante 17
Centro ①
+34 917 553 926
www.60balconies.com

This new building in cool Almirante, built by 60 Balconies, is completely in line with their core concept, offering a flat that could be a design flat of a local. Each apartment is decorated in its own style. Their spaces have also become an art gallery with original artworks for sale.

430 **MATUTE 11**

Plaza de Matute 11
Centro ②
+34 609 354 982
www.matute11.com

Located in a modernist palace in Madrid's Letras district, just a few steps from Santa Ana Square. The building was renovated between 2010 and 2015. It is a personal project of Marga Pérez, a specialist in design and rehabilitation of spaces.
The 25 apartments are spacious and individually decorated, creating unique spaces with their own personality.

427 **GRAN VÍA CAPITAL**

MADRID RÍO

30 WEEKEND ACTIVITIES

The 5 best **FLEA MARKETS** ———————— 220

5 wonderful **BIKE TOURS** in Madrid ———————— 222

The 5 best places for
BEAUTY AND MASSAGE ———————— 224

5 **DAY EXCURSIONS** outside Madrid ———————— 226

5 **SWIMMING POOLS** to cool off
during the summer ———————— 228

5 places to practise **YOGA AND PILATES** ——— 230

The 5 best

FLEA MARKETS

431 **EL RASTRO**
Calle de Toledo
Centro ②

El Rastro is Madrid's most popular open-air flea market. It is organised in La Latina every Sunday from 9 am to 3 pm.
It has been the place to go for over 400 years for many curious objects. Head to the antiques and specialised shops around La Ribera de Curtidores for more interesting finds.

432 **MERCADO DE MOTORES**
AT: MUSEO DEL FERROCARRIL
Paseo de las
Delicias 61
Arganzuela ⑧
*www.mercado
demotores.es*

This market, which is held on the second weekend of the month (except in August), is located in the Ferrocarril Museum spilling out onto the adjacent lot. This flea market invites local shops and artisans to showcase their products as well as individuals who have found treasures in their attic. Great vintage clothing and furniture.

433 **NÓMADA MARKET**
Plaza de la Cebada
Centro ②
*www.nomada
market.com*

This market, first organised in 2005, takes place one weekend every two months.
It aims to be a platform for the work of emerging designers: fashion, accessories, illustrations, jewellery, furniture, lighting, footwear and stationery.

434 MERCADO PRODUCTORES

Matadero Paseo
de la Chopera 14
Arganzuela ⑧
+34 622 255 851
www.mercado
productores.es

On the last weekend of the month, this market is the best place to meet the producers and farmers of the Community of Madrid. Here you can taste and buy local organic products. A great place to discover the local Madrid gastronomy and learn more about it.

435 MERCADO CENTRAL DE DISEÑO

Matadero Paseo
de la Chopera 14
Arganzuela ⑧
www.mercado
dediseno.es

For one weekend every month, except in January and February. The Matadero is a showcase of national and international designers in a festive environment with plenty of music and good food. With 600 square metres dedicated to design, concerts and street food trucks, there is plenty to see and do.

431 EL RASTRO

5 wonderful
BIKE TOURS
in Madrid

---

436 MADRID BICI
www.infobicimadrid.es

You can find these bikes almost everywhere in the city. If you are an occasional user, just follow the instructions on the display at the bike station. The bikes are half electric making your bike trip even easier. Download the app to see how many bikes are available at any given station.

437 MADRI RÍO
Arganzuela ⑧

Madrid's equivalent of New York's High Line but bigger and greener. Along the Manzanares River a 30-km cycling path (shared with pedestrians) also connects to the 'Anillo Verde' (Green Ring), the cycling path that encircles greater Madrid. In summer, Madrid Río becomes an urban beach.

438 CASA DE CAMPO
Moncloa-Aravaca

The park has a 17-km route created especially for cyclists. It borders the entire perimeter of the park and includes emblematic points of interest such as the Antequinas stream, the House of Cows and Covatillas hill. Take a 2-hour tour and enjoy the biggest green park of the city.

439 **PALACIO REAL**

Plaza de Oriente
Centro ②

Bike to Plaza de Oriente where you can see the Opera house, the Royal Palace and Almudena Cathedral. Continue your tour towards Parque del Oeste and make a quick stop at the Debod Temple to admire the views of Casa de Campo Park.

440 **PARQUE FELIPE VI**

Valdebebas

Parque Felipe VI, in Valdebebas district, used to be agricultural land but has since been upgraded. Since it is not yet very known, you might well be the only person biking through the 470-hectare park. This beautiful landscape design combines vegetation and trees that are typical of the centre of the Iberian Peninsula.

437 MADRID RÍO

The 5 best places for
BEAUTY and MASSAGE

---

441 NATURA BISSÉ SPA
AT: HOTEL URSO
Mejía Lequerica 8
Centro ①
+34 914 444 458
www.hotelurso.com

Located in the luxury boutique hotel Urso, the spa offers treatments by Natura Bissé, a Spanish beauty brand. Together they have developed a special and exclusive ritual to oxygenate your skin. Combine it with a series of facial and body treatments, and you will feel absolutely rejuvenated after two hours of relaxation.

442 THE ORGANIC SPA
Lagasca 90
Salamanca ③
+34 915 775 670
www.theorganicspa
madrid.com

Claiming to be the first organic spa in Europe, this place offers a selection of beauty treatments - facial and body. They excel at traditional Thai massages and other techniques from Balinese massages or the Hawaiian Lomi Lomi. The facilities are very elegant and are the perfect place to unwind.

443 ISAAC SALIDO
Villalar 11
Salamanca ③
+34 915 762 175
www.isaacsalido.es

What makes this space so unique, is that it does not look like a beauty salon (and even less like a hairdresser's). Yet it is 100% dedicated to beauty, wellbeing and enjoyment. Along with a Japanese food and cocktail bar (NikONikO), this hedonist space, designed by hairdresser and stylist Isaac Salido, will surprise you.

444 TACHA

Castellana 60
Salamanca ③
+34 915 612 433
www.tacha.es

Located in an impressive space, this haven of beauty is dedicated to caring for women: hairdressing, beauty treatments, make-up and massages. A beauty salon that is drenched in natural light with an outstanding architectural design. Many Spanish celebrities rely on the expert hands of Natalia de la Vega.

445 HANDMADE BEAUTY

Conde de Xiquena 17
Centro ①
+34 913 196 610
*www.handmade
beauty-db.com*

A beauty shop and manicure salon that works with natural and organic products only. They offer vegan manis and pedis, suitable for pregnant women and people with celiac disease. Charming interiors with antique chairs and light colours. They also formulate their own brand, which is available to buy.

443 ISAAC SALIDO

5
DAY EXCURSIONS
outside Madrid

---

446 EL ESCORIAL
www.el-escorial.com

Located 45 km to the northwest of Madrid, you can get here by bus from Moncloa. The village was named after the impressive and majestic monastery. Initially built as a mausoleum for King Philip II and his family, it was also designed to commemorate the battles he won against the Frenchmen in Picardy.

447 SEGOVIA
www.turismo desegovia.com

About 90 km north of Madrid, Segovia in the Castile and Leon region, is a world heritage city. Stroll down pedestrian streets, see the famous Roman aqueduct and the cathedral as well as the 11th-century Alcázar Palace, where Queen Isabel agreed to finance Christopher Columbus's adventures.

448 TOLEDO
www.toledo-turismo.com

This World Heritage city is located about 70 km south of Madrid and can be easily reached by train from Atocha station. Also called the city of three cultures, as Christians, Muslims and Jews lived together there for centuries. Toledo was also the home of the painter El Greco.

449 EL PARDO ROYAL PALACE

www.elpardo.net

This palace was built in the 16th century, inheriting some elements from the original medieval structure over which it was built. Check the opening hours before going, as this palace has also been used as accommodation for visiting heads of state since 1983. Bus line 601 from Moncloa.

450 ARANJUEZ

www.aranjuez.com

Declared a World Heritage Cultural Landscape by UNESCO, you can easily get here, by bus, from Estación Sur (a 50-minute journey). Visit the majestic Royal Palace, which was built in a Renaissance and neo-Classical style. Don't miss the gardens with their fountains. The Palace is very large and will take a while to visit.

5

SWIMMING POOLS

to cool off during the summer

---

451 **GYMAGE LOUNGE RESORT**
Luna 2
Centro ①
+34 915 320 974
www.gymage.es

Gymage is a social club and gym with an exceptional rooftop terrace, restaurant, cocktail bar, sun deck and a nice little infinity swimming pool. The pool is open to club members and to the public. Check their website for the fees and conditions.

452 **UNIVERSIDAD COMPLUTENSE**
Obispo Trejo 8
Moncloa-Aravaca
+34 913 941 174
www.ucm.es/piscina-de-verano

This swimming pool only admits students and professors (bring a student card). The only other way is to get in is as a guest of a student. That means there are no children or rowdy families. Here everybody is young. You will have to pay a 5 euros entrance fee to enjoy the Olympic pool and gardens.

453 **MELIÁ BARAJAS**
Avenida de Logroño 305
Barjas
+34 917 477 700
www.melia.com

If you are looking to beat the summer heat and escape the city, then take a taxi to Meliá Barajas hotel (on the way to the airport, just 15 minutes out of Madrid), which has a very nice pool and garden. For 30 euros you get access to the pool, lunch in the garden restaurant and a towel.

454 ÁREA RECREATIVA DE RIOSEQUILLO

Carretera Madrid-
Irún, Km. 74
Buitrago del Lozoya
+34 912 932 047

The artificial lake of Riosequillo is located 80 km to the north of Madrid and has fantastic views over the Sierra. The swimming pool is surrounded with gardens and trees, and is a lovely place for a picnic. It gets pretty crowded on summer weekend with families.

455 LAS BERCEAS

Piscina Natural
De Cercedilla
Cercedilla
+34 918 525 740
*www.cercedilla.es/
las-berceas*

Las Berceas would have been a perfect backdrop for a Slim Aarons photo in the seventies. Located 60 km northwest of Madrid, the scenery here is unique. Nestled in the middle of a natural park in the mountains of Dehesas and surrounded by pine trees, this is a natural pool with no chemicals to treat the water.

5 places to practise
YOGA and PILATES

---

456 AYOGA

Atocha 56
Centro ②
+34 653 717 005
www.ayoga.es

This is the first centre in Madrid that offers different disciplines of traditional and contemporary yoga in one space, including Hatha, Vinyasa, Kundalini, Yin Yoga, aerial Yoga, Pilates and even yoga for children. They charge a fee of 15 euros for a trial lesson. You can buy 10-lesson passes or pay a monthly fee.

457 ZENTRO URBAN YOGA

Claudio Coello 5
Salamanca ③
+34 635 822 237
www.zentroyoga.com

ZUY is one of the pioneering urban Yoga centres in Spain. Its first studio opened in 2005. At the Madrid studio, they offer classes in various Yoga disciplines, Pilates and Mindfulness. A class costs 18 euros. The website lists all the options available if you want to continue taking classes.

458 BIKRAM YOGA CENTER

Barquillo 38
Centro ①
+34 913 192 058
www.bikramyoga
center.es

Solely dedicated to Hot Yoga, the Bikram Yoga Center has a solid reputation with Yoga practitioners but also with actors, artists and singers. One of the first centres to open in 2009, it remains loyal to its core concept. 25 euros per class and several options if you want to take more classes.

459 ELIZA COOLSMA

San Lorenzo 20
Centro ①
www.elizacoolsma.com

She used to be an editor for a fashion magazine but then, one day, she was ready for a change. After years of practising and learning various Yoga techniques, she now teaches Flow classes. She organises Meetups (in English) at the Wunderhouse for up to 21 participants. First time 5 euros and 12 euros for every next single class.

460 ESTHER HUERGA

Don Ramón
de la Cruz 64
Salamanca ③
+34 910 176 156
www.estherhuerga.com

Specialising in Pilates and Hypopressive Abs, Esther Huerga teaches classes in her studio, with Pilates reformers. Classes are either individual, with a friend or in a group of up to 4 people. She combines mat and reformer in her classes. 80 euros for a session with a friend.

456 **AYOGA**

40 FACTS
ABOUT MADRID

5 **FESTIVITIES** *not to miss in Madrid* —————— 234

5 **MOVIES** *filmed in Madrid*————————— 236

The 5 most important **HISTORIC FACTS**
about Madrid————————————————— 238

The 5 most curious **STREET NAMES** —————— 240

5 **BLOGS** *in English about Madrid*————————— 242

5 *facts you should know about* **THE METRO** ——— 244

5 *anecdotes about* **FAMOUS PEOPLE** ————— 246

5 **NOVELS** *set in Madrid* ——————————— 248

5
FESTIVITIES
not to miss in Madrid

461 LA ALMUDENA

This religious festival is celebrated on November 9th, in honour of the Virgin la Almudena, one of the patron saints of the city of Madrid (along with Saint Isidro and la Paloma). Nuestra Señora de la Almudena is a small wood statue, depicted holding the baby Jesus. The Madrilenians pay tribute to her during this simple religious ceremony.

462 SAN ISIDRO

On May 15th, Madrid celebrates the feast day of its patron saint. Tradition dictates that you start out the day on San Isidro esplanade where thousands of people enjoy a picnic. Followed by an afternoon bullfight in Las Ventas, during the most important bullfighting festival of the world, and ending the day dancing el chotis during the many open-air dances that are organised in the old quarter.

463 VERBENA DE SAN ANTONIO DE LA FLORIDA

This festivity, which is celebrated on June 13th, has a religious component, which is the benediction of bread for the poor. The popular component developed in the 19th century. Unwed women offered 13 pins to the saint, in hopes of finding a husband during the next year. The festivity ends with open-air dancing.

464 VERBENA DE LA PALOMA

During the month of August, Madrid's city centre celebrates a trilogy of festivities dedicated to San Cayetano, San Lorenzo and ending with La Paloma on the 15th. This last open-air celebration with street food and dancing has its origins in a portrait of the Virgin, which was found by nuns in 1787.

465 EPIPHANY – THE 3 KINGS

In Spain, Epiphany is more commonly known as the feast of the three kings. It is celebrated on the evening of January 5th, with huge parades all around the city, welcoming their Eastern Majesties, who will leave presents for good children and coal for those who were less good that night.

5

MOVIES

filmed in Madrid

---

466 THE BOURNE ULTIMATUM (2007)

Some of the scenes in the third instalment of this franchise about an agent with amnesia, played by Matt Damon, were filmed in Madrid. The Café del Principe in Canalejas square is the place where a journalist (Paddy Condisine) meets with Madrid's CIA chief. Bourne later escapes from a flat in Virgen de los Peligros Street followed by a spectacular car chase through Castellana.

467 DÍAS DE FÚTBOL (2003)

Besides the actors, one of the other characters in this hilarious Spanish comedy, is the neighbourhood of La Elipa. Centring around subsidised housing apartment blocks, built between 1960 and 1970, the film depicts the local football pitch, the nearby pinewood picnic table and the neighbourhood's long-standing request for a metro station in the form of graffiti with the slogan 'Metro Ya'. The metro station was finally built in 2007.

468 THE GOLDEN AGE OF HOLLYWOOD IN MADRID

Stars like Charlton Heston, Ava Gardner, Sophia Loren, John Wayne and Bette Davis were received by crowds of fans, with flower bouquets and paparazzi when they landed in Madrid. In the fifties and sixties, the visionary American producer Samuel Bronston filmed epic movies around Madrid and in his massive studios in Paseo de la Habana 68, which were comparable to Hollywood's MGM or Paramount.

469 DOCTOR ZHIVAGO (1965)

Madrid was chosen by director David Lean to recreate Moscow on a 20.000-square metre set around Silvano Street. A vacant waste lot was completely transformed in just five months with snowy streets, a streetcar with a line of houses that were built just for the occasion as a backdrop and a fake Kremlin to transport us to pre-revolutionary Moscow.

470 SOME MADRID FILM SETS OF ALMODOVAR'S FILMOGRAPHY

Montalban 7, the attic on the seventh floor where Pepa (Carmen Maura) lived in *Women on the Verge of a Nervous Breakdown* (1988). Plaza de Santa Ana 15 (Villa-Rosa), where Miguel Bosé performed as a transvestite in *High Heels* (1991). Eduardo Dato 18, where the couple played by Javier Bardem and Francesca Neri lived in *Live Flesh* (1997).

The 5 most important
HISTORIC FACTS
about Madrid

---

471 THE CAPITAL AND THE AUSTRIAS

In June 1561, Felipe II wanted to move the court, to escape from the influence of the Archbishop of Toledo. He chose to settle in Madrid because it had a good climate and excellent hunting grounds. The city's central geographic position in the Iberian Peninsula and the fact that Queen Isabel de Valois adored Madrid played a big part in his decision, too.

472 THE FIRST BOURBONS AND THE ENLIGHTENMENT

With the fourth Bourbon, Carlos III, Madrid finally evolved from a city in La Mancha, to a modern European capital. The King, who was widely considered the best mayor Madrid ever had, gave the city public lighting, running water and a sewage system as well as numerous majestic buildings and a court with plenty of splendour.

473 THE WAR OF INDEPENDENCE (1808-1814)

The treaty of Fontainebleau in 1807 allowed Napoleon's troops to cross into Spain to attack their joint enemy, Portugal. But this was just a manoeuvre to occupy Spain. On 2 May 1808, Madrid revolted against the French, and although the revolt was contained, it marks the uprising of the rest of Spain and the start of the War of Independence.

474 THE BATTLE FOR MADRID, SPANISH CIVIL WAR (1936)

In November 1936, several strategic villages on the outskirts of Madrid were occupied by General Franco's National Forces, who were prepared to take Madrid. The trade unions and political parties mobilised Madrid's population with the slogan '¡No Pasarán!' (They shall not pass!). With the help of the International Brigades (Russian tanks and planes), Madrid resisted the siege.

475 THE 23F

On 23 February 1981, Colonel Tejero and his men invaded Parliament, holding the representatives of the legislative and executive powers as hostages and compromising the recently achieved democracy. The Palace Hotel in front of the Parliament served as the operational headquarters for dealing with the situation, which ended some time past midnight, with the King's televised speech.

The 5 most curious
STREET NAMES

476 CALLE DEL CODO (ELBOW STREET)
Centro ②

The 70-metre-long street connecting Plaza de la Villa with Calle del Conde De Miranda possibly takes it name from its 90-degree-angled shape. It is said that the 17th-century writer Quevedo always chose this gloomy alley to urinate when he got back home from his usual nights of heavy drinking.

477 CALLE DE LA LECHUGA (LETTUCE STREET)
Centro ②

This short street that connects Calle de El Salvador with Calle Imperial is believed to be almost 500 years old. Many authors believe its name comes from the fact that it used to be the location of a daily market where farmers from around the Manzanares river and from Aranjuez sold their vegetables.

478 CALLE DE LA PASA (RAISIN STREET)

Centro ②

A popular saying in Madrid is: 'El que no pasa por la Calle de la Pasa no se casa' (He who doesn't walk up Raisin Street can't get married). This saying was inspired by the fact that the Palace of the Archbishop of Madrid was located on this street. That was where you came to do the paperwork when you wanted to get married.

479 PESADIZO DEL PANECILLO (BREAD PASSAGE)

Centro ②

This alley connects the episcopal palace with the church of San Miguel and its name comes from the custom of the Archbishop of Toledo, Luis de Borbón y Farnesio (1727-1785), who gave bread to each beggar that knocked on the window of his residence, which was located in this street.

480 CALLE DEL DESENGAÑO (DISILLUSION STREET)

Centro ①

Goya lived at no. 1 from 1779 and 1800, in what is one of the oldest streets in Madrid. Its name was inspired by a rather absurd legend. Two gentlemen about to duel are distracted by a shadow and forget about their dispute. They decide to follow the shadow, only to realise with great disillusion that it was actually a dead body.

5
BLOGS
in English about Madrid

---

481 NAKED MADRID
www.nakedmadrid.com

Launched by an international group of Madrid enthusiasts, this is a very well laid out and nice-looking blog. It has in-depth reviews about Madrid's restaurant and bar scene, as well as tips about activities or day trips to the surrounding areas. They also provide useful services for expats to get settled.

482 MADRID COOL BLOG
www.madrid coolblog.com

Sandra, Rebeca and Angel launched this very honest project sharing their passion for very special restaurants, shops and bars around the city of Madrid and some great weekend trips to take around Spain. It has a useful map to filter the information and an English version.

483 MY LITTLE MADRID
www.my-little-madrid.com

This regularly updated blog about new and fun things to do around the city by two sisters, Almudena and Marcela de la Peña, is a great example of a blog that has also evolved into a guide of Madrid. You will find information about bars, restaurants, shops and the city's cultural scene, both in English and in Spanish.

484 OH HELLO, SPAIN

ohhellospain.
blogspot.com

This is a very personal blog by British expat Kate Turner. It's not only about Madrid but also about her trips around Spain. With great insights on what to do and see in Madrid, it's not really a directory but rather a good place to learn a bit about what's it like for an expat to live in Madrid.

485 MUCHBITES

muchbites.com

The British author Wesley Munch grew up in Milton Keynes, developing a passion for food and eating. After spending a year studying in Madrid, he became frustrated that he couldn't find the real local places and temples to food. That is why he decided to launch a blog to help other foodies find the next best culinary experience.

5 facts you should know about
THE METRO

---

486 BUILT IN 3 YEARS AND INAUGURATED IN 1919

Construction of the first Metro line began on 19 September 1916. Three years later, on 17 September 1919, Line 1 was inaugurated by King Alfonso XIII. On the official picture he had his eyes closed and the photographer painted them in afterwards. They look exaggeratedly open. The journey took 10 minutes and a ticket cost 75 cents.

487 DIRECTION OF THE METRO: FROM LEFT TO RIGHT

This is one of the most common questions that Metro users ask. The reason why the Metro arrives in the station from the left is due to the fact that in 1919, when the Metro was inaugurated, vehicles drove on the left side of the road in Madrid. This only changed in 1924.

488 TODAY IT'S THE 7TH LONGEST METRO LINE IN THE WORLD

With a 300-kilometre network and 13 lines, this is the seventh longest metro in the world, carrying close to 600 million passengers each year. Line 1 has the most stations (33) and Line 12 is the longest with 41 km of tracks.

489 GOYA ENGRAVING

One of the most curious metro stations is Goya. The station is profusely decorated with the engravings of Goya from his series of Caprichos, one of his finest works, with its satirical presentation of society's follies, which also depicts various bullfighting moves that were popular at the time.

490 PALEONTOLOGICAL BONES FOUND WHEN CONSTRUCTING CARPETANA STATION

In 2008, during the excavation works to install new elevators in Carpetana metro station on Line 6, 15.000 fossils from the middle Miocene period were found. The station has a small museum with replicas of some of the 15-million-year-old fossils, including a wolf-bear, a giant dog, a mastodon and a rhinoceros.

5 anecdotes about
FAMOUS PEOPLE

---

491 CHE GUEVARA

In 1959, young Ernesto Guevara travelled to Madrid twice. He went to a bullfight in Las Ventas, visited Complutense University and walked around the centre of Madrid visiting la Favorita, the oldest and most prestigious hat shop in Madrid. He bought an Elósegui brand beret, made in Tolosa, Spain (his famous beret).

492 ERNEST HEMINGWAY

In the fifties, Nobel Prize laureate Ernest Hemingway visited Madrid, lured by the food and the bullfights. He spent a lot of time with his friend bullfighter Luis Miguel Dominguín and Ava Gardner at the Cervecería Alemana in the heart of Santa Ana Square. This German beer bar is more than 100 years old and for generations has attracted bullfighters and bullfighting fans.

493 **AVA GARDNER**

The beautiful Hollywood diva lived in Madrid from 1952 to 1967 partly because of her romance with bullfighter Luis Miguel Dominguín. She lived by her own rules and enjoyed Madrid's nightlife with great excess and passion. She was kicked out of the Ritz Hotel for questionable behaviour and set up residence instead in the Castellana Hilton, the present-day Intercontinental Hotel.

494 **FRANK SINATRA**

In 1956, Frank Sinatra accepted a role in a movie shot in El Escorial, hoping to rekindle his romance with Ava Gardner, who was living in Madrid. So he picked up the phone one night and sang at the piano to her for one hour. When he finished, there was nobody at the other end. Ava was actually standing right behind him, she had driven all the way just to be there with him.

495 **ARISTOTELES ONASSIS**

When Aristoteles Onassis visited Madrid with Maria Callas in 1953, they had drinks at Chicote Museum, the cocktail bar where famous writers, Hollywood actors, royals and anybody who was somebody got together. Pedro Chicote showed them his private collection of liquor bottles. It was so valuable that Onassis offered him 2 million dollars for the lot but Chicote refused.

5

NOVELS

set in Madrid

---

496 LEAVING THE ATOCHA STATION
BY BEN LERNER

This first novel by poet Ben Lerner tells the story of a young American poet on a fellowship in 2004. He came to Madrid to research a poem about the Spanish civil war but ultimately it became more of a voyage of self-discovery. Discovering Madrid and the world that surrounded him, he witnessed the aftermath of the 11M terrorist attack.

497 FORTUNATA Y JACINTA
BY BENITO PEREZ GALDÓS

There is a widespread consensus that this masterpiece by Benito Perez Galdós is the most important fiction novel written in Spain after *El Quijote*. The life and activities of Madrid's late 19th-century middle class society is perfectly represented in this story that unfolds around two main characters who lived in the area around the Plaza Mayor.

498 **MUCHO TORO**
BY TIM PARFITT

This is an exaggerated and hilarious comedy about an expat's view of Spanish idiosyncrasies. In the late eighties, Tim Parfitt arrived in Madrid to launch the Spanish edition of Vogue magazine. What originally was meant to be a six-week stay ended up being nine epic years in Madrid.

499 **WINTER IN MADRID**
BY C.J. SANSOM

This historical novel is set in the 1940s during the aftermath of the Spanish Civil War with Madrid in ruins. Harry Brett, a veteran of Dunkirk, is sent out by the British Secret Service to gain the confidence of his old school friend Sandy Forsyth, now a shady businessman.

500 **CAPTAIN ALATRISTE**
BY ARTURO PÉREZ-REVERTE

This series of nine novels by Arturo Pérez-Reverte narrates the adventures of Captain Alatriste, a veteran who survived as a mercenary in 17th-century Madrid. The novel is a realistic portrayal of the Spanish Golden Age, a period during which arts and literature flourished, coinciding with the political rise of the Spanish Habsburg dynasty.

INDEX

1862 Dry Bar 77
60 Balconies Recoletos 217
A Punto 117
A&G Madrid 55
ABC Museo de Dibujo
    e Ilustración 173
AC Palacio del Retiro 215
AC Santo Mauro 209
Álbora 41
Alipio Ramos 88
Amazonico 47
Amen 103
Andres Gallardo 113
Angel Sierra 88
Angelita 85
Anglomania 107
Antigua Casa Crespo 120
Antiguo Museo
    del Ejército/Salón
    de Reinos 134
Apodemia 112
Aranjuez 227
ArcoMadrid 190
Area Recreativa
    de Riosequillo 229
Arima 53
Aristocrazy 112
Arzabál 37
Aspasio Boutique
    Apartments 216
Ayoga 230
BA&SH 110
Babelia 47
Baby Deli 199
Bacira 59
Bajo El Volcán 128
Bar Cock 90

Bar Martin 84
Barajas Terminal 4 139
Barbanarama 96
Barra /M 51
Barrio de las Letras 154, 178
Basílica San Miguel 184
Batavia 118
BBVA Las Tablas 138
BD Madrid 119
Bearbie 96
Benares 169
Bibo 48
Big Mamma 129
Bikram Yoga Center 230
Billiesmarket 202
Bio in the Bowl 32
Biombo 13 105
Bistronomika 59
Blanche & Mutton 127
Boa Mistura 166
Bodega de la Ardosa 87
Bodegas Ricla 87
Bonnet à Pompon 202
Boquadillo de Jamón
    y Champagne 39
Bosco de Lobos 36
Brumalis 114
Café de Chinitas 182
Café Moderno 95
CaixaForum 175
Calle del
    Doctor Fourquet 179
Cannibal Raw Bar 54
Cartujano 121
Casa America –
    Cien Llavas 80
Casa Ciro 30

Casa de Campo 222
Casa Décor 190
Casa Labra 42
Casa Lucio 42
Casa Patas 182
Casa Perico 44
Cazador 99
Celicioso 67
Centro Cultural
    Conde Duque 179
CEPSA Tower 139
Cervantes y Compañia 117
Cervecería
    Santa Barbara 84
Cha Chá The Club 81
Chamberí 154
Chifa 60
Church of San
    Andrés Apóstol 185
Church of San Antinio
    de los Alemanes 185
Church of San Manuel
    y San Benito 184
Church of Santa
    Bárbara 185
Cinco Jotas 40
Cine Doré 189
Cine Estudio 189
Cines Renoir Retiro 188
Círculo de Bellas Artes 75
Ciudad Real Madrid 160
Coconut Bar 94
Colegiata e Instituto
    de San Isidro 134
Copenhagen 34
Corazón 94
Corral de la Morería 182

osette 108
Costello Café
   & Nite Club 180
Costello Río 197
Cripeka 24
Cristina Oria 63
Crucina 35
Crustó 25
Cuervo Store 128
Dear Hotel 207
Dear Hotel –
   Nice to Meet You 74
Del Diego 92
Delirio 97
Des Petits Hauts 111
Do Design 102
Don Juego y
   Don Puzzle 198
Dray Martina 50
Dry Martini 91
DSTAgE 48
Ecoalf 104
Edificio España 143
Edificio Metrópolis 143
Ekseption 108
EL 91 107
El Escorial 226
El Ganso 106
El Horno de Babette 65
El Huerto de Lucas 29
El Imparcial 169
El Invernadero
   de Los Peñotes 30
El Junco 180
El Mirrador del Thyssen 36
El Moderno 102
El Paracaidista 102
El Pardo Royal Palace 227
El Pelicano 80
El Penta Bar 158
El Porrón Canalla 38
El Quinto Vino 86
El Rastro 220
El Retiro 150, 151

El Sol 158
El Tulipán 161
Eliza Coolsma 231
Eltono 167
Embassy 63
Epiphany –
   the 3 kings 235
Eric Vökel Apartments 216
Espacio Fundación
   Telefónica 174
Estación de Atocha 145
Estadio Santiago
   Bernabéu 160
Esther Huerga 231
Faunia 194
Federal Café 26
Filandon 197
Fismuler 31
Fit Foot 32
Flamingos
   Vintage Kilo 131
Florida Retiro 52
Fonti 26
Fortuny 82
Frida 36
Fulanita de Tal 97
Fundación Carlos
   de Amberes 162
Fundación Francisco
   Giner de los Ríos 175
Fundación Juan March 174
Fundación Mapfre 175
Ganz Café 26
Gastañer 121
Glent 120
Gorila 98
Graf 82
Gran Mélia Palacio
   de los Duques 208
Gran Vía Capital 216
Guillermo
   de Osma Galeria 176
Gymage Lounge Resort 228
Habanera 47

Handmade Beauty 225
Hanso Café 71
Helga de
   Alvear Galeria 176
Hotel 7 Islas 207
Hotel Emperador 210
Hotel Tótem 207
Hotel Único 206
Hotel Urban 211
Hotel Urso 208
Hotel Wellington 210
How 118
Huerto de las Monjas 152
Hyuro 166
IKB 191 130
Il Tavolo Verde 35
Imaginarium 198
Isaac Salido 224
Ivorypress 177
Jardines del Palacio
   del Príncipe
   de Anglona 152
José Alfredo 91
Joselito's 40
Juanita Cruz 46
Kikekeller 92
Kiki Market 32
Kilñmetros de Pizza 196
Kulto 51
L'Atelier Óptica 125
La Almudena 234
La Bicicleta 98
La Bobia 159
La Boulette 40
La Cabaña Marconi 196
La Candelita 56
La Carmencita 58
La Casa del Pez 93
La Casa Encendida 178
La Casa Tomada 38
La Castela 57
La Central – El Bistró 73
La Dolores 44
La Duquesita 62

La Fabrica 72
La Fábrica de Camisas 168
La Fabrica
   de Maravillas 83
La Garriga 38
La Integral 128
La Jefa 27
La Lupita 56
La Magdalena
   de Proust 33
La Mejor Tarta
   de Chocolate
   del Mundo 61
La Melguiza 63
La Mona Checa 130
La Movida 168, 169
La Raquetista 58
La Riviera 180
La Tape 83
La Vasqueria Montanesa 31
La Vía Láctea 158
Lago 119
Lamucca 49
Lander Urquijo 106
Las Berceas 229
Las Salesas 155
Lateral Castellana 79
Lavapiés 155
Lavinia 86
Levadura Madre 65
Libreria Desnivel 116
Lolo Polo 62
López Pascual 41
Los Kioscos of
   the Florida Retiro 196
Macchinine 199
Macera 77
Madreat 28
Madrid Bici 222
Madrid Fly 195
Madrid Me Mata 159
Madrid Río 222
Madriz Hop Republic 83
Magasand 24

Magpie 130
Maje 110
Makkila 49
Malababa 113
Mallorca 24
Mama Campo 33
Mamita 81
Man 1924 106
Mantequeria Bravo 64
Margarita Se
   Llama Mi Amor 114
Marieta 45
Martina Cocina 25
Martínez Bar 94
Masscob 104
Matadero Madrid 178
Matute 11 217
ME Madrid
   Reina Victoria 215
Meet 103
Meliá Barajas 228
Mercado Central
   de Diseño 221
Mercado de Motores 220
Mercado Productores 221
Mesón Txistu 161
Mestizo 118
Microteatro por Dinero 186
Ministerio de Asuntos
   Exteriores 134
Mint&Rose 121
Moby Dick 181
Modernario 131
Monasterio
   del Corpus Christi 135
Mondo Galeria 176
Moss Floristas 115
MOTT 109
Motteau 61
Mulafest 191
Murillo Café 30
Muros Tabacalera 167
Museo Chicote 90
Museo de Cera 200

Museo del Ferrocarril 20■
Museo del
   Romanticismo 17.
Museo del Traje 20■
Museo Nacional Centro
   de Arte Reine Sofía 17:
Museo Nacional de
   Ciencias Naturales 20:
NAC 10■
Naif 9■
Nanos 20■
Natura Bissé Spa 224
Navaja 16■
NH Casa Suecia 21■
NH Collection Colón 21■
Nicoli 20■
Nitty Gritty 37■
No Name 6■
Noisés Pérez
   de Albéniz 177
Nómada Market 220■
Nubel 52■
O'Pazo 54.
Ocho y Medio
   Libros de Ciné 73
Ochoymedio 96.
One Shot Hotel 168
Only You Boutique
   Hotel Madrid 206
Óptica Caribou 127
Óptica Toscana 125
OTTO 80
Palacio de Cibeles 145
Palacio de Cristal 145
Palacio de
   Fernán Núñez 163
Palacio de Liria 163
Palacio de los
   Duques de Uceda 135
Palacio Longoria 162
Palacio Real 223
Panic 65
Panta Rhei 116
Parque de el Capricho 149

arque del Oeste 148
arque Felipe VI 223
arque Juan Carlos I 148
arque Quinta
  de los Molinos 149
asajes 116
equeño Cine Estudio 188
errachica 45
ez 109
hoto España 190
lanthae 115
laza de la Paja 152
laza de la Villa
  de París 153
laza de Oriente 165
laza del Ángel 153
laza Mayor 136, 137
ointer 46
rado Museum 138, 172
raktik Metropol 212
uerta de Alcalá 142
uerta de Felipe IV 141
uerta de Hierro 141
uerta de Toledo 142
uerta Real 141
um Pum Café 71
unto MX 56
Quadra Panis 67
Radio City 129
Rayén Vegano 34
Real Jardín Botánico 149
Ritz 27
Ritz Madrid
  (Mandarin Oriental) 214
Rocambolesc 62
Room 007 213
Room Mate Óscar 210
Sala Clamores 181
Sala de Despiece 51
Salamanca 155
Salmón Gurú 76
Salon des Fleurs 70
Salvador Bachiller 75
San Antón 29

San Ginés 44
San Ildefonso 28
San Isidro 156, 157, 234
San Miguel 29
Sanchis Bar
  Marisquería 160
Sandro 110
Sanguchón 39
Sanissimo 34
Santamaría La Coctelería
  de al Lado 93
Sasha Boom 59
Scalpers 105
Segovia 226
Siroco 81
Sleepn Atocha 213
Sport Hielo 195
Stop Madrid 88
Street Art 166, 167
Suarez 112
Sueños Polares 203
Swinton and Grant 72
Taberna Gaztelupe 53
Taberna Pedraza 58
Tacha 225
Tasca Celso y Manolo 57
Tatel 45
Teatro Calderón 186
Teatro de la Zarzuela 186
Teatro Lara 187
Teatro Luchana 187
Terraza Suecia 74
The Dash 76
The Hacienda
  Warehouse 85
The Hat 212
The Kooples 111
The Metro 244, 245
The Organic Spa 224
The Principal – Terraza 74
The Principal
  Madrid Hotel 208
The Robot Museum 201
The Westin Palace 215

Tienda Poncelet 64
Tiendas Así 198
Tipos Infames 72
Tiradito & Pisco Bar 55
Tirso de Molina 114
Toledo 226
Toma Café 70
Toni2 91
Torres Bermejas 183
Torres de Colón 139
Tupperware 95
UHostel 212
Ulloa Optico 125
Ultramarinos Quintin 79
Universidad
  Complutense 228
Urkiola Mendi 53
V Manneken 77
Vacaciones 99
Vailima 70
Válgame Dios 92
Veranos de la Villa 191
Verbena de la Paloma 235
Verbena de
  San Antonio
  de la Florida 235
Villa Magna 209
Villa-Rosa 183
Vino y Compañia 85
Warner Park 194
Whitby 49
Wunderhouse 162
Yelmo Ideal 188
Yipi Yipi Yeah 166
Zentro Urban Yoga 230
Zoo Aquarium
  of Madrid 194
Zubi Design 104

COLOPHON

EDITING *and* COMPOSING — Anna-Carin Nordin

GRAPHIC DESIGN — Joke Gossé and Sarah Schrauwen

PHOTOGRAPHY — Neima Pidal — www.neimapidal.com

COVER IMAGE — secret nr. 501: Cuesta de Moyano, Retiro

The addresses in this book have been selected after thorough independent research
by the author, in collaboration with Luster Publishers. The selection is solely based
on personal evaluation of the business by the author. Nothing in this book was
published in exchange for payment or benefits of any kind.

D/2017/12.005/4
ISBN 978 94 6058 2066
NUR 506

© 2017, Luster, Antwerp
www.lusterweb.com — www.the500hiddensecrets.com
info@lusterweb.com

Printed in Italy by Printer Trento.